FOUR FOR THE KING!

The Inspiring Story of All-American Running Back Brian Pruitt

BRIAN PRUITT

ISBN 0-9770144-0-1

Dedication

This book was written in loving memory of my grandparents Luterry and Ceola Pruitt. In the past few years there hasn't been one day that I haven't longed to hear your voices or see your smiles. You were truly the heart and soul of the Pruitt family. Everything that we are or ever will be God has birthed through you. Thank you for showing us true character, integrity and love. See you on the other side.

Love Brian and the rest of the Pruitt's

Special Thanks

The Brian Pruitt story would have been a tragic one without the following people who I would like to thank.

Thanks to my beautiful wife Delicia "We did it Honey!" You have been my encouragement, editor and entertainer while writing this book. Your love for me has been proof of God's favor on my life. You are my sunshine! I'm looking forward to spending the rest of my life with you and showing the world what we can accomplish together.

To my Mother everything that you have given will sooner or later come back to you. Words can not express my love for you. Watching you I've learned that if I never quit I can't lose.

To my big sister Stephanie "The Champion" thanks for looking out for a little bad boy. You carried the weight for me as kids and I will never forget.

To my big brother and mentor Mike McMorris, you have been an excellent example. I wish every kid in America could spend one day with you, it would change their life like it did mine. You have shown me the meaning of hard work and that dreams are attainable.

Thanks to the Pruitt family Tanisha Pruitt, Terry Pruitt, Carolyn Pruitt, Dawn, Dena and Dana Pruitt, Marilyn Pruitt, Gwen Pruitt-Harris, Mike Pruitt-Dixon, Harold Pruitt, Kenny Pruitt, Suzan Pruitt-Hunter, and Carol Walker my God-Mother.

To Lawrence McKinney, you have been a father to the fatherless for years. You have left a legacy of love, an example of responsibility, a shadow of servant-hood and gained many sons. I love you dad!

To Pastor James and Leona Glenn and Center of Attraction Church, I wouldn't have made it without you and your guidance. You have taught me the value of wisdom. My life is evidence that you are touching the world. Thanks for allowing me to eat from the table of your life.

To Brian Molitor and family you have been my extended family, friend and mentor. I want to thank you for helping me with the writing of this book over the past seven years. Even more thanks for making your home a place of refuge for me and for speaking into my life. I'm forever grateful.

To Pastor Ron and Carla Ives and the Potters House church, you taught me character and integrity. You invested in me and loved me as your own as a family and a church. You were my strength and a place of refuge through my college days.

To the Mostek Family Bob, Diane and my brother Jeff – 1991 was the start of a beautiful friendship that I pray will never end.

To the Mid-American Champs of 1994 Central Michigan Chip's. I learned the meaning of the word "Team" from you. I will never forget the friendships we made.

To Coach Herb Deromedi, Dick Flynn, Tom Kearly and the Central Michigan coaching staff for giving me a chance to prove myself in the classroom and on the field.

Finally to Youth Nation and Kingdom Shakers. I want you to know that I have learned more from you than you will ever learn from me.

CONTENTS

Introduction

It was 1977, and I was four years of age when I came to the realization of what was happening on my mother's television set. It seemed to me as if on that Sunday afternoon the Dallas Cowboys and the Washington Redskins were in an all out war. At that point I wasn't sure if I wanted to join the army or play football, but being on a battlefield seemed overwhelmingly exciting. Hypnotized by the intensity of the game and the hype of the commentators, I slowly put my G.I. Joe toys down. I paid so close attention, that nineteen years later I still vividly remember this childhood story. After watching a few quarters of the game my mind was made up; the army wasn't for me but football was. At that moment it felt like time stood still as I walked over to my mother and said, "That's what I'm going to do mama; I'm going to grow up and play football!" Eighteen years later my mother explained to a curious young man why she decided to name him Brian. My mother told me that years ago she was deeply touched and impressed by a movie entitled "Brian's Song." To my knowledge this was a movie that told the story of a heroic football player. Little did my mother know that someday a sequel would be made to "Brian's Song." For destiny had also given Brian Pruitt a song to sing. My mother never knew that somewhere in the future, a place unknown, the world would dance to a song we later knew as, "Four For The King!"

CHAPTER 1
A Long
Awaited Moment

The ball was on the five-yard line with fifty seconds to go in the game. Every person in the stadium was on their feet and screaming at the top of their lungs. To my right there was a sea of fans dressed in orange and white cheering for the hometown team, the Bowling Green Falcons. The Falcons fans were calling us names I dare not repeat. To my left was a mountain of maroon and gold worn by our Central Michigan University Chippewa's faithful fans. Both teams' fans were waiting to see who would get to charge the field and chant. "We're number one!" In front of me lay the path to my dream, the Mid-American Conference Championship. My teammates and I were five yards and fifty seconds away from being the MAC Champions -- or from going home in disgrace.

My quarterback, Eric Timpf, called us all into the huddle as he struggled to dislodge the muddy grass that was wedged between his helmet and his facemask. My teammates' eyes were as big as silver dollars. This was not the look of fear but the look of hunger. We were hungry for a win after coming off of two losing seasons. To us, the end zone represented a buffet. Eric called the play, and to no surprise I would be receiving the ball. At that point in the season I was competing for the title of the nation's leading rusher, which made Bowling Green's defense key in on me even more.

Suddenly, one of my linemen began to motivate himself by grunting as fast and hard as he could. I was afraid that he was having a heart attack! In the cool autumn air, steam rose from his head in great white plumes. He quickly turned his head towards me and through his tightly gritted teeth he snarled, "Follow me to the end zone, Pruitt!" Clinching his fist, he promised that he would trample the guy across the line from him. I winked and promised, " I'll meet you in the end zone!"

Next, our quarterback barked out the order that the ball would be hiked on "three". Then he yelled, "Ready!" In response, we yelled "Break!"

Players from both teams approached the line of scrimmage and stared across at the face of the enemy. The crowd erupted into a deafening roar. Off to my left, I could hear a group of players on our sideline chanting, "Four for the King! Four for the King! Four for the King!"

Bowling Green's defensive players were slapping each other across the helmet and screaming that "nobody was going to get into their end zone." Suddenly, Eric took his position behind center and yelled, "Down!" Our offense slowly and painfully went down into position. Sixty minutes of violent collisions with our opponents had taken their toll on us. "Hut one!" Shouted Eric.

I looked across the line of scrimmage and saw both linebackers were staring straight into my eyes. Today, they weren't just members of the opposing team. Instead, they were obstacles standing in the way of my dream. For a moment, it seemed that time stood still. My mind raced back to another football game that had taken place hundreds of miles away. I was instantly filled with painful memories of that championship game played a decade earlier in Saginaw, Michigan. On that day, my team had lost and the rival fans charged the field in celebration. I could suddenly feel the agony of that loss and the chilling realization that if I failed in the next few seconds, I would feel that horrible feeling of defeat once again...

I was suddenly jolted back to the present when I heard my quarterback yell, "Hut two!" Thoughts of the past two losing seasons burned like fire as every muscle in my body tightened for what I knew was to come. The noise from the crowd was deafening by this point. Faintly I heard my quarterback say, "Hut three!" as the ball was hiked.

Players on both sides of the line smashed together with ferocious impact. The collision of helmets, shoulder pads, and unprotected skin sounded like a plane crash. Mud shot up into the sky from cleats digging deep into the war-torn ground. Players grunted and screamed in hopes of finding the strength needed to dominate their opponents on what could be the last play of their collegiate careers.

Just as Eric took the snap from our center and sprinted towards me to hand off the ball, a huge defensive lineman slipped through a gap and dove to tackle him. Miraculously, Eric was able to place the ball into my waiting hands just before he was smashed to the ground by the enormous lineman. I quickly shifted my view toward the gap in the line only to see another defensive lineman racing towards me. Instinctively, I sidestepped him and was launched like a rocket toward my dream. A dream that began years earlier when I was a young boy growing up on the mean streets of Saginaw, Michigan...

Team Huddle #1
Questions and Answers!

1. What is your dream for your life?

CHAPTER 2
In The Beginning

It was third and long that wet, humid day. I was an eight-year-old speedster proud to be playing football with the teenage bullies in my neighborhood. As we gathered around our quarterback, I heard him call a play. The plan was for me to run up the sideline as fast as I could and catch the winning touchdown pass. Filled with excitement, I lined up in my wide receiver position. I kicked my foot to plant it in the ground, wiggled my fingers, then turned and gave my defender the eye. Soon, the ball was hiked and I made my move. The young defender slipped and I flew past him heading for the end zone. My Quarterback faked a run and then launched the ball high into the air. Everything was just perfect! I remember thinking to myself, "I'm going to be just like the guys on TV. I'm going to catch this ball, score the touchdown and be a star. I'll show the older guys that Brian Pruitt can play with the best of them"! Soon, the ball was coming down as I fought off another defender, kept my concentration, and made a circus catch on the run. As I headed down the field, my hopes of being the star of the game were seconds away from being reality. Suddenly, just inches from the goal line, three different guys hit me and sent me flying. Sadly, I didn't land in the end zone. Instead I landed in a four-foot ditch full of dirty water. All the neighborhood kids had a good laugh that day as I dragged my wet, aching body home.

Many kids would have been too scared or embarrassed to go back to that field, but not me. In fact, while growing up in Saginaw, Michigan, most of my time was spent in the streets, on a basketball court, or in a football field competing against older kids. I wasn't naive enough to think that these guys were really my friends. They only let me play football with them so that they could have somebody to play "kill-the-man" with. They would give me the ball and just see who could hit me the hardest. Believe me; when everybody on the field is trying to tackle you, the phrase, "running scared," becomes a reality.

Strange as it sounds, there were actually some good things happening within me during this time period. Somewhere in all the fear, unfair odds and unbeatable opponents, several key aspects of my life began to take shape. I sensed that some day in the future, the painful lessons learned in humiliation and failure would give way to courage and victory. It was as if an unseen hand guided me during this challenging part of my life's journey.

Building A Foundation

Later that year, I was involved in my first organized sports competition. My cousin, Mike, got me involved in running track in the Friendship Games. Mike was my only male cousin, and we both were the same age. So we thought of ourselves as brothers more than cousins. The Friendship Games consisted of organized competition between young athletes from Saginaw and Sault Ste. Marie, Canada. To me, the Friendship Games were great! One year, we would go to Canada for a weekend of friendly competition and the next year the Canadians would come to America. I can remember staying with some of those Canadian families and how they went out of their way to make us feel at home.

The Friendship Games allowed us to have good competition and develop great relationships. My cousin and I had great success at these games. We never failed to take first or second place in all our races for many years in succession. We'd bring our medals home and show them off to the other kids in the neighborhood. Then we would challenge them to a race in order to prove that we were the best. To this day, I thank God for such an organization. The Friendship Games helped build a foundation of confidence within me, yet despite all of the success, medals and recognition, I realized that I was still lacking something. I just did not know what it was.

The Lack of a Father

Looking back on my early years, I have to admit that I had a terrible attitude. One day I was kind to other people and yet, the next day I didn't care if anyone else existed. Deep inside, I really did have a big heart; the problem was my big heart had a big hurt. This big hurt was growing up without a father. It was rough living in a single parent home. Growing up, my hero was my older sister Stephanie. Stephanie had the awesome responsibility of trying to keep me out of trouble. My sister was a very high spirited person, and I could tell that her little brother meant the world to her. We both had the same mother but different fathers. Our mother, Joyce, was and is a strong lady who looks five years younger then her age and is truly a wonderful lady. Because she was a single parent trying to provide for her family, we didn't get to see her as much as we would have liked. Stephanie and I both cherished the time that we did have with her and truly loved our mother. However, my sister and I did not have the same feelings towards our fathers. Even now the memories of these men bring me pain rather than peace.

I remember the first time my sister's dad came to the house to pick her up for a visit. My sister was dressed really nice and was so excited. Because she was excited I got excited too...even though I had no idea what we were so excited about. All of a sudden someone came to the door. My mother answered, and a very tall man walked in. Just then my sister grabbed her coat, ran, jumped into this man's arms, and with a smile on her face yelled "Daddy!" Soon, they were headed out the door and I began to panic. I thought I better hurry and grab my coat if we were leaving. I ran for the door, but my mother grabbed me and told me that I couldn't go. I remember kicking and screaming because I wanted to go too. She tried to explain to me that the man was my sister's dad and not my dad. In other words, he was not responsible for me. At that point, I asked the one simple question that mercifully had never been asked before. "Momma, where is my dad?" Silence filled the room. That was a strange moment for my mother and me. There I was six years old and for the first time in my life a very foreign word came out of my mouth. The word, "Dad." My mother later told me that she had dreaded the day that she would have to explain my father's absence. She tried her best to explain to a curious little boy why his father wasn't around, but no matter what she said, I couldn't understand.

I walked away from the conversation crying. Feelings of rejection and abandonment motivated every tear. As I sat on the top of my stairway, a time bomb was planted deep within my soul. Formed in minutes, it would take years to finally defuse. The bomb was called anger. My feelings of rejection and abandonment led me into a dark world of rage that smoldered deep within. On those rare occasions that the bitterness subsided, I felt totally worthless. These dreaded emotions tainted everything that I did. Often, I would make bad decisions out of anger, venting my frustrations on my sweet mother, who did everything she could just to take care of my sister and me. Later, those same frustrations spilled over into society.

The Cruelest Blow

As the years went on I learned about my father from my mother, family and friends. Not much of what they told me was good. One day, my mother told me that he was a very abusive man. As she spoke, tears flowed down her cheeks as the pain of a painful past overflowed. Still, I didn't want to believe the negative things that she or anyone else said about my father. In my mind, I created an image of him that was everything that I needed. No, my dad was not mean; instead he was loving, kind, and compassionate. He loved me unconditionally. My father didn't really leave me; he was just gone for a while. Some day everything would be just great between us. Sadly, reality hit me one day when the phone rang. I answered deepening my voice, trying to sound as grown up as possible. On the line came an unfamiliar voice that caused my heart to race with these simple words. "Hello Brian, this is your dad." At that moment I felt the same excitement my sister did when her father came to see her. I knew that everyone had lied about my father. He didn't leave me; he had only been gone for a little while! Those six little words brought an incredible peace to my young soul. He was just like I always imagined him to be. Suddenly my mother entered the room and asked me who was I talking to on the phone. With great pride I said, "My dad." Her reaction shocked me. Instantly fire rose up in her eyes and she looked like a mother bear trying to protect her cub. She quickly took the phone away from me and asked my father what he wanted.

I confidently waited by my mom's side knowing that dad would explain that he had come back to be with me-- his son. In my young mind, I could picture him walking through our front door, catching me as I jumped into his arms and then carrying me on his shoulders toward a great time together. Unfortunately, that scene was never to be. What happened in the next few seconds shattered my dreams and exposed the true character of my father. As soon as he heard my mother's question, he erupted like an angry volcano. The calm voice that I had heard moments before, began screaming so loud that it seemed that he was standing right there in our living room. Waves of paralyzing fear swept over me. I wanted to hide in a corner. Then my father made the statement that would change our relationship forever. I very clearly heard him scream that he would rather see me dead than to be with

11

my mother. My mother replied that if he ever harmed me in any way, that she would not put him in jail, but bury him underneath the jail. Then my mother demanded that he never call again and slammed the phone down.

On that sad day all my fantasies about my father were shattered. Instead of being my provider, protector and my friend, he was mean, scary, and a bully. In some ways I was happy he wasn't in my life. Not only did he reject us and beat my mother, but now he's threatening my life. Sadly, I was forced to accept that my father was everything my mother and family had said that he was. That night was restless. I tossed and turned in my bed thinking about the threat my father made towards me and wondered if he would carry it out. Seeds of fear, combined with bitterness and anger, continued to grow inside of me.

Bad Attitude and Wrong Friends

Shortly after that night, I was walking home from school and tried to pick a fight with one of the neighborhood kids. I was not aware that an older woman sitting out on her porch watched the whole thing. The other boy failed to respond to my profanity-laced challenge, so I began to walk away thinking I was cool. Just then that old woman came down from her porch and said to me, "Your attitude is so bad that it's going to get you into some serious trouble. It might even get you killed one day!" Instead of listening to her voice of experience, I rudely told her to shut her mouth along with a few other things that I am ashamed of today. As the years went by I began to fulfill what that old lady said. Looking back, I don't know who was worse, my enemies or my friends. All of them were bad news. It wasn't until years later that I realized just how dangerous some of those people were.

Betrayal and Revenge

Growing up, I had a hard time determining who my real friends were. So many of the people that I hung around with couldn't be trusted with anything of value. I remember one day that several of the local boys came over to the house to show me their new boxing gloves. The new gloves belonged to two of the meanest kids in our neighborhood. They were twins who were always in trouble. My friend Don was also there. We were all excited to try the gloves on and find out who the toughest kid was. After a few hours of beating one another silly, the twins suggested that we take the brawl to Don's house. They said that we could get an extra pair of gloves and that way, everybody could box.

Well, as we got on our bikes to leave, the twins lied and said that they needed to go home first, but that they would join us shortly. Don and I waited at his house for hours and the twins never came. Finally, I decided to go home. When I got there, my mother was standing at the door with a look of disgust on her face; a look that I had seen too many times. As I stepped into the house, my worst fears were confirmed. My mother told me that we had been robbed—once again.

Growing up, our house was constantly invaded by robbers. This was very frightening for a young boy with no father in the home. The scariest part for me was that my mother always slept on the living room couch. Our house was designed so that a person had to go through our living room to get to any other part of our house. This meant that when robbers would break in they had to walk right past my mother before they ransacked our home. She had to pretend that she was asleep and pray to God that they wouldn't hurt her or her children. I still remember hearing strange noises in the night, and then rushing to my window to see the shadow of robbers fleeing into the darkness. Times like that made me feel scared and helpless. I was scared for my family. I felt helpless because I knew that there wasn't much that I could do to protect my sister and my mother. After all I was the only man that my family had. I never could figure out what they were coming for, because we never really had much of anything worth stealing. A small radio or our old television was usually the target of these night time raids. That summer day after our boxing match was different. Strangely enough, this time all the robbers took was food. Every cabinet in the house had been cleaned out, and all that was left in the refrigerator was a small box of baking soda. I looked down and lying next to the refrigerator was a clue to the identity of the robbers -- the jacket of one of the twins. I couldn't believe that they robbed my house. It didn't surprise me that they would steal, but I couldn't believe that they would steal from me. After seeing the jacket, it was easy to figure out what had happened. The twins had pretended that

13

they were going home, but instead they returned to rob my house. Amazingly, they broke in, stole all our food and were stupid enough to leave one of their jackets behind. I decided to tell my mother the story of how my friends had robbed us. She went and got her belt and whipped my butt, not because someone else stole something, but because I wasn't supposed to have anyone at the house in the first place. That day I vowed in my heart that the twins wouldn't get away with stealing from Brian Pruitt's family. They would pay and pay dearly.

For months I looked for a way to get back at the twins and finally it happened. One day as we were leaving school I saw a crowd of people standing in a circle that usually meant that there was going to be a fight. I decided to see what was going on. As I made my way through the crowd, I saw a wonderful opportunity. The twins were about to jump on this guy, Ken. I looked into Ken's eyes and saw that he was terrified. He knew that the twins would attack him like piranhas and devour him in seconds. I quickly put my book bag down, jumped in the twin's face and told them to leave Ken alone. I also said that I knew they had robbed me and that's why I hadn't been hanging out with them. Then I pulled Ken aside and told him this was a perfect opportunity for both of us. We could fight the feared twins, one on one, that way neither one of us would have to worry about being jumped by the other. I asked Ken if he agreed and it took all the strength he had just to say yes. It was quite clear to me that Ken wasn't going to be much help, but I figured it would be better than fighting alone. I turned towards the twins. Thinking that I had Ken's support, I walked up and pushed one of the twins. At this point there was no turning back. I got in my fighting position as they started coming at me. All of a sudden I heard a loud scream, "Mama!" and the sound of someone running. I turned and saw Ken running home screaming for his mother.

Then the fight began. All I could remember were all the things my mama said as she whipped my butt for letting the twins rob us. I fought like a man on a mission. I fought for my mama's groceries. We fought for nearly two hours, the whole school stood in a circle watching to see who would be the last one standing. The crowd was cheering me on, "Brian! Brian!" This was mostly because I was doing what they were all afraid to do-- fighting the feared twins. That day, it was an anything goes fight. That meant that you did what you had to do to win. I found that out as one of the twins kicked me in the face as I pounded his brother. I was determined that nothing would stop me. I moved like a cat, and I felt as strong as a lion.

It turned out that I was just a little too much for the twins. I was too strong, too fast, and most of all… they had stolen my mama's groceries! That day I whipped them the same way my mama whipped me, very convincingly. As I walked home all the kids at school treated me like a hero. I was now the cream of the crop. I fought the neighborhood bullies and lived to tell the story. By the time I got home I was badly bruised, but I was holding my head high. I was the man! More importantly, I felt like I got my mama's groceries back. Shortly after the big battle with the twins, my mother moved my family to the other side of town. The good news was that I was still able to attend my old school. The bad news was that I took my bad attitude to the other side of town with me and made more enemies.

Does Race Really Matter?

After moving to the other side of town, I found myself without a friend for months. I would go outside, sit on my porch and watch the other kids play. The neighborhood kids seemed to be very shy. After a few months I made two life-long friends by the names of John and Blu. John was a little skinny redhead with a lot of spunk. For lack of a better term, my buddy, Blu was just plain big. People always thought he was older than his actual age of ten.

There was something different about my new neighborhood. Most of the people living there were white. In this new environment, I discovered something that never mattered in my old neighborhood -- I was black. Up to that point in my life, I didn't know that there were people who thought that there was something wrong with being black. It soon became clear that some white people had problems with the color of my skin, especially since I lived in their neighborhood. Over the next few years the majority of the fights that I got into were over racial issues. Amazingly, some of the kids that I fought with in the neighborhood later told me that they had looked down on me because they heard their parents doing it at home.

One day Blu came over to my house out of breath and very

upset. My mother and I sat Blu down to ask him what was wrong. With tears in his eyes, he told us that as he was heading to my house a police officer stopped and asked him if any "niggers" lived in the neighborhood. My friend simply asked him why. The cop went on to say that blacks were "bad news for good neighborhoods". He said that blacks wanted everything without working for anything. The officer concluded by saying that blacks weren't interested in doing anything educationally to improve themselves. Blu said that he was so scared he wanted to wet his pants. He also said he was so angry he wanted to punch the cop in the face. Fortunately for my friend, he did neither. Instead, he decided to call the cop a liar and run.

My mom and I could tell that this event really confused Blu. Like me he was young, naive, and learned from his mother that all people were equal regardless of their color. On that sad day Blu found out that not everybody believed as we did. Situations like this made life scary in my new neighborhood, but that event only made the bond between my friend and I greater. We felt as if we had a mutual secret the rest of the world didn't seem to know, and that was that all men were created equal.

As life went on my friendships with John and Blu became priceless. They taught me that not everybody was out to get me and that there were people in the world who would judge me on my character, rather than the color of my skin.

More Than A Coach

By the time I was in the fifth grade, I had thought up clever ways to vent my anger without getting into any legal trouble. My most ingenious way was trying out for elementary sports teams. I remember trying out for the fifth grade basketball team. I walked into the gym where the try-outs were being held and saw a man standing in the corner with twenty kids jumping all over him. At that moment I had two questions. Who was this man? Why was everybody acting like he was special? As the weeks went by my questions were answered. This gentleman's name was Lawrence McKinney and he was the basketball coach. Yes, he was special, but time would tell just how special for a young man like me.

Lawrence was not only a coach; he was a father figure to hundreds, if not thousands of kids. He had been coaching at

Heavenrich Elementary School for many years. Anybody who knows Lawrence will tell you that there has never been a day that he hasn't tried to make life better for some kid. Little did I know that day when I walked into that gym that this man would make a great impact on my life.

I believe Coach McKinley was placed in my life for many reasons but two of them really stand out to me. The first reason was to teach me to stop feeling sorry for myself. He taught me that just because life had seemed to deal me a bad hand, this wasn't an excuse to throw my life away. Growing up without a father had left me feeling rejected and angry. Lawrence made it clear that this wasn't a good reason not to leave my mark in history. From our frequent talks, I learned that countless young people faced the same hurdles of rejection and abandonment that I faced growing up without a father. Unfortunately, these negative emotions swallow many of them up. Anger causes their dreams to be blurred by pain, bitterness, and unforgiveness.

The second reason I believe that Lawrence was in my life was to help me build my self-esteem. Coach always saw me as a real person and not just an athlete. He was just as concerned about the development of my character as he was about my physical talents. His input was crucial in the development of Brian Pruitt as a person. He told me that there were many pro athletes who possessed tons of talent and only a pinch of character. This imbalance eventually destroys them. Coach taught me that no matter how talented I was, I still needed to allow life's circumstances to build the character within me to be ready for what lay ahead in my future.

During this crucial time, I learned that there were three things needed to survive in the inner city. First, you needed to be involved in extracurricular activities in order to stay out of trouble. Second, you needed a dream or a vision that someday you were going somewhere to do something great. Finally, you needed someone like Lawrence to make you believe that those dreams could be accomplished.

I still get tears in my eyes when I reflect upon two life changing conversations I had with Lawrence many years ago. The first took place on a Saturday evening while we were watching television at his house. We began to talk about some pretty deep issues that night. At one point, Lawrence asked me if I knew where my

17

father was. Because I had no answer, the room became very silent. In that moment, fear gripped my heart. I was afraid because the friendship that I had built with Lawrence suddenly began to demand my trust. This was a problem, because I had never really trusted a man before. Lawrence, in his own gentle way, began to move me out of my fear. We had a long conversation that day about the man I never knew, my dad. At the end of our time together, I had shed many tears and opened my heart for the first time ever. Mercifully, Lawrence gave me permission to call him "dad". The things that were spoken to me on that day began a healing process that would allow me to grow into a man.

The second conversation took place after I had tried out for a local summer basketball team, only to be cut. The coach of that basketball team clearly showed favoritism when picking his players. After the final cut, the entire team was made up of players from the school where he regularly coached. I went to all the tryouts and thought that I did really well. On the last day of the tryouts, I decided I would go to practice early. I wanted to be well prepared to assure myself a spot on the team. When I got there the coach wouldn't open the door despite the fact that he was standing right next to it. For over an hour I kept knocking until he finally opened the door.   The coach grabbed me and told me I couldn't make the team because I had come to practice late. I was furious at the unfairness of the situation and that there was nothing that I could do about it. That was the first time I had failed at making any sports team. When I saw Lawrence that night, he noticed that I was really discouraged. He asked me if I had made the team. I told him the embarrassing truth about how I had been cut. Lawrence gave me his undivided attention as I was speaking knowing this was a crucial point in my development as a person as well as an athlete. When I was done telling my story, Lawrence began to speak as if he had been to the future and back. He said there would be a day when colleges from all over the nation would do anything to get me to come to their schools and play whatever sport that I wanted. He told me that one day America would hear my name mentioned with the nation's top athletes. Lawrence believed in me, but more importantly Lawrence got me to believe in myself.

The story that destiny was writing about Brian Pruitt, was not being written on paper or being written by pen. It was a story being written on my heart by men of character, and integrity like Lawrence. He began taking me to local high school sporting events. After each game, my mentor would always say, "Someday that's going to be you out there playing and I'll be in the crowd watching." Times like that gave me vision, courage and a destiny. Even after I grew into the next phase of my life, my relationship with Lawrence never changed. I entered into my middle school years with renewed self-esteem and believing in myself like never before. Lawrence, the first father figure I ever knew, was kind, compassionate, and loved me unconditionally. Thanks dad.

Team Huddle #2
Questions and Answers!

1. Based on the comments of those closest to you how would you rate your attitude?

   Excellent – I keep a good attitude on a consistent basis.

   Good – I am usually positive and think before I act.

   Average – My attitude greatly depends on how I feel on that given day.

   Poor – I have a bad attitude.

2. My most painful experience in life was the absence of a father. What is the most painful experience of your life? If another person was involved, what would you like to say to this person if you could see them today?

3. Are you willing to forgive the person that you refer to in question number two?
   > If your answer is yes, then what would your statement of forgiveness sound like?
   >
   > If your answer is no why not?

4. Who does your lack of forgiveness hurt the most, the other person or you?

5. Do you believe that all people are equal regardless of their race or gender? Why or why not? How does your answer shape your relationships with others?

CHAPTER 3
Learning Some Important Lessons

Bad Grades and Bad Decisions

My first two years in junior high school weren't much fun, especially when it came to academics. I failed my seventh grade year and then barely made it through my eighth grade year. By that time, my poor study habits and lack of interest in school became obvious to all of my teachers. In fact, I failed so many classes that I had to retake them instead of moving on with my classmates the following year. I was humiliated to learn that by not applying myself, I had fallen out of the graduating class of "91" and into the class of "92". The thought of this made me the butt of a lot of jokes and really hurt my feelings. I felt stupid knowing that I could have done the work, but just never did it.

Lack of studying was not the only bad decision that I made during this troubled time. I started hanging out with one of the local drug dealers who went by the name of Big "C". Big "C" was about twenty years old, dressed sharp, drove nice cars, and had more money and jewelry than anyone I had ever known. Looking back, I think that the thing that drew me to him was that he accepted me at a time when everyone else thought that I was stupid. Big "C" drove me around in his nice cars and slipped me money all the time. He made sure that I had nice clothes and jewelry as well. He made me feel cool, especially when he would pick me up from school. All the kids would stand in awe of his Cadillac and loud music. The car would roll up with its gold rims and music so loud you could always hear him coming from blocks away. When the kids saw me with Big "C", I no longer felt stupid -- I felt cool.

It took some time for me to realize that Big "C" was leading me down the wrong path of life. He had been an outstanding high school football player from the southern states. He was big, fast and strong. Even at the age of twenty and not having played football in years, Big "C" was still built like a truck. The truth was, even though it looked like he was cool, he wasn't. Big "C" never went on to college and he didn't have a job, not a real job anyway. The worst part was that he was destroying his community with drugs. That was definitely not cool. Before long, his luck ran out and he joined thousands of other criminals— behind iron bars.

One day while making a drug deal, Big "C" got caught. I was thankful that I wasn't with him. Actually it was a miracle that

I wasn't, because we were together every other day that week! When the cops arrested him, Big "C" had so many illegal things in his possession that he spent the next nine years in jail. After Big "C" went to jail I went back to being plain old me. That was all right with me, because after seeing what happened to the "cool" drug dealers, one thing was for sure, I never wanted to end up behind bars. So, I swallowed my pride and returned to school, this time committed to make it work.

A Big Boost From A Big Brother

During this time in my life I was introduced to a very important person. My mother was always coming up with ways to make sure I was going to have good influences around me. She, therefore, enrolled me in the Big Brother - Big Sister Program. This was an awesome program that connected adults who were willing to spend their time with needy youth like me.

When I found out that my mother had placed me in this program, I was so excited! I was going to have an older brother. After signing up I was placed on a long waiting list. This list was full of kids whose parents, like mine, thought that they needed help. After what seemed like a year, my mother received a call informing her that they had found a match for me. His name was Mike McMorris.

My imagination was running wild as I sat slightly scared and yet filled with great expectation. This was the day that Mike and I would meet for the first time. What would this Mike guy look and be like? Would I like him? More importantly would he like me? While waiting, my mother decided to calm her nerves by grooming me profusely. Suddenly there was a rapid knock at the door. Boy was I thankful! This was my chance to escape my mother's grooming death grip. My Mom rushed off to greet my new big brother, and I trailed slowly behind her as if she was my shield from evil. There he was: A good-looking college student at Saginaw Valley State University. Mike's big smile and great people skills seemed to put my mom at ease right away. As for me, it was going to take just a little bit more than that to earn my trust. The good news was that Mike was up for the challenge.

Mike and I found out that we had a lot in common. One of them was karate movies. We spent the rest of the evening watching karate movies and eating homemade milk shakes.

I had the time of my life! It was almost too good to be true. Mike was not only a match for me but he was the perfect match for me. Mike was a goal setter, and he set those goals very high. I listened to him share his life's dreams and then one by one I watched him accomplish them. Discipline, hard work, and teacher were the words that most describe my big brother. Mike would take me on road trips all over the place. He always took every opportunity to teach me about life and academics. My brother Mike, in my opinion, was and is god sent. I had a renewed sense of doing and being the best that I could be.

I spent my second try at seventh grade hitting the books. There was no way that I was going to fail again and become part of the class of "93". While I didn't get all A's, my grades did greatly improve. Suddenly, when the teachers asked a question I would raise my hand to answer. Other students began to look to me for some answers. That was a real shocker for someone who had failed these same subjects just months before! My time with my big brother, Mike, was greatly paying off.

One day, in the middle of that school year, I was called down to the principal's office where the school counselor was waiting to see me. I had never been to see the school counselor before and thought that this was serious! I sat down in the chair in front of the counselor's desk with a "what-did-I-do-now?" attitude. He sat back in his chair and flipped open a big yellow folder that had my name printed on it. He then pulled out two report cards and began to quietly compare them. I sat in silence hoping to God that he wasn't going to tell me that I was now going to become a part of the class of "93". Just then the counselor pushed his glasses firmly against his face, leaned over his desk towards me and asked me if I believed in second chances. My reply was, "That depends on what I get a second chance to do." After all, since I was experiencing my second chance at the seventh grade, I knew that seconds weren't always good. At that moment, the counselor smiled and told me to relax. He went on to say that because of my academic improvement, the school was willing to move me up to the eighth grade for the next semester. Now that was a second chance I was willing to take! The counselor made it very clear that I would have to keep up with the work or there would be some serious consequences. I was willing to take that challenge!

When the second semester started, there I was in the eighth

grade as proud as could be. It took me a year and a half to make it, but I made it. It felt great sitting in class with my friends and no longer being the butt of jokes. I did it! With a little hard work and some studying I jumped back into the graduating class of "91".

Good Friends

While in Junior High School I developed close relationships with two new friends. The first friend I met was Willie. Willie and I had a lot in common when it came to football. We both had dreams of making it big someday and selling our brand of Starter jackets and gym shoes in stores all across America. Also, Willie and I both had a tough-guy complex and would wrestle to see who was the strongest. During the first few weeks of the school year, the upper classmen had what they called "slop day." Slop day was a day of initiation for all freshmen. This initiation time involved various forms of punishment that ranged from emotional to physical. Willie and I had made up our minds from day one that we were not going to run when the upper classmen came for us. We made a commitment that not only were we not going to be slopped, but that we would slop anyone who came after us. Sure enough, lunch-time came and the upper classmen were chasing lower classmen all over the school grounds. Kids were crying, screaming and trying to find a place to hide. It sounded like war had broken out on our school grounds! As Willie and I were walking down the street, a large group of the upper classmen noticed us. The moment of truth arrived and our commitment was about to be tested.

We heard footsteps running towards us as the pack of seniors rushed forward. We both looked at each other as if to say "do we really want to go through with this?" The answer on each of our faces was certainly. Willie and I stood our ground that day. Not only did we stand our ground, we won that ground and the respect of all the upper classmen. Side by side Willie and I kicked, bit, scratched and screamed. Like two cowboys, we wrestled that herd of upper classmen and rounded them up. After the upper classmen saw how well we handled ourselves, they offered us the opportunity to be on their side. Exhausted from the big brawl, we decided to join them. I am embarrassed to say that for the next few weeks Willie and I joined the upper classmen in beating, robbing and terrorizing the lower classmen. Needless to say, students in our grade level knew us as traitors, but at that time being known as a traitor was far better than having to fight the entire upper class again!

The second friend I met was a young man by the name of Eric. Eric and I had a lot in common when it came to basketball. We both had dreams of being on the highlight reels of the NBA commercials. On weekends we would take his parent's video camera outside and tape our dunks. After taping all our best dunks, we would go back into the house and analyze every move to see how we could improve them. After all, a dunk had to be sweet if it was going to be on TV. Eric and I had the privilege of being the stars of our Junior High basketball team. The big question back in those days was who was the better player between the two of us?

One day the coach set up a one-on-one tournament for the twelve guys on our basketball team. For the next three hours it seemed like the NBA finals were taking place in our gym. We weren't team members any more. Everyone's pride was on the line. One by one, guys started dropping out of the competition. Guess who were the two last men standing? You're right! My buddy, Eric and me. The first player who scored eight points would win the championship game. Each basket counted as one point and three pointers only counted as two points. We each played that game like we were the worst of enemies. Eric had his crowd rooting for him, and I had my crowd rooting for me. When I look back on that time, I can remember how tired and beat up we both felt. The funny thing is, I don't even remember who won the game. If anyone were to ever ask me, I would say I won the game, only because I know that Eric would probably say that he won!

During those times, friends like Willie and Eric made life fun and exciting. However, years later I came to understand the role that they played in my destiny. You see in those early years at junior high, I began to branch out and play basketball, soccer, floor hockey, baseball, and track. The problem was that by getting involved with all of these other sports, I lost my desire to play football. Little did I know that my friends Willie and Eric would soon play a major role in setting me back on course toward my destiny.

Team Huddle #3
Questions and Answers!

1. Do you consider yourself to be a good decision maker?

   Why or why not?

2. If "birds of a feather flock together," then what type of people are you spending time with?

3. Are your friends flying in the direction of your goals?
   If your answer is no, then how will this affect your dream?

CHAPTER 4
Positive Peer Pressure

By the time I entered the ninth grade, I hadn't played any football in over two years. However, since it was the beginning of the school year, everybody was planning to try out for the football team. This was especially true of Willie and Eric. They couldn't stop talking about it! One day while having lunch, my friends tried to persuade me to try out for the football team. By the time we finished our sandwiches they had convinced me to join in on the fun. I remember going to the first practice and trying to hide behind my two buddies, because I felt so strange around the other guys.

The coach of our team was Coach Jim Jones. Coach Jones was a very tall and well-built man who, at one time, was an outstanding college football player. To us, Coach was a star because he had played at such high levels. The thing that I liked most about Coach Jones was that he would always race against the players after practice was over. He was always trying to see if he still had it. His competitiveness and intensity rubbed off on his players. Coach was always there to pat you on the back when you did well, but also to make you run endless laps if you didn't. I really liked his balance and the fact that you always knew what he was thinking. His thin, stern face would let you know when he meant business and his big smile told you when to be at ease.

As the weeks went by, I not only made the team, but I also was given a starting position. Coach Jones said he made me a starter because I ran faster than anyone on the field. What he didn't know was that I ran fast because I was afraid. I remembered what it was like to get tackled! But fear was not the only emotion that was rekindled that year. Just being on the field brought back memories of my childhood dream.

The Championship Game

Our team played well all season. So well that we found ourselves tied with our cross-town rivals which meant that we would face them in a one game showdown for the title. This championship game would involve the two most feared teams in the city league, the Central Cougars and my team, the North Vikings. Central had a line up of great athletes such as T-Mac, Jamie Lay, Tree and Tank. T-Mac was a star at the receiver position. Jamie Lay was an elusive speedster at quarterback. Tree was nothing less than what his name stated. He was tall and could reach to the sky when a pass was thrown his way. Tank, much to the sorrow of our defense, was a 210-pound monster running back.

The North Vikings were not without their own weapons either. We had Eric Harrison, Willie Rogers, Jason Mazola, and one scared running back-- me. Eric was our quarterback; Willie and Jason Mazola were both feared at the linebacker positions. And, I was our number one running back.

I remember how excited and nervous I was to be playing in the city championship game. I also remember how frustrated I was, because I had to keep going to the bathroom every few minutes--after I had put all of my equipment on! By the time the game started, I was physically and emotionally drained and we hadn't played a down yet!

Just before the game, both team's coaches had a chance to meet at midfield. I don't know what was said that day but when Coach Jones came back to the sidelines he was not a happy man. The opposing coach had insulted him. Our game plan changed from running the ball to the outside to running inside of our tackles. The whole game was just straight running the ball up the middle, something that we had not done all year. It seemed as if Central's coach had pulled some reverse psychology on us and had us playing their game. It was brutal! On one play, their big ball carrier came running toward the sidelines trying to run my buddy Eric over. Instead, Eric picked him up and slammed him into a trashcan out of bounds.

When we had the ball, Central's defense, The Purple People Eaters, was on full throttle. It seemed like there was no escaping those guys! One play, I tried to run the ball up the middle only to have two guys grab me and power slam me to the ground. The hit was so brutal that the game literally stopped as coaches ran toward my motionless body. Pain nearly overwhelmed me, snot ran down my face, and courage tried to flee my heart. Looking back, I see that was a moment of truth for me. It was the moment that I had to either let go of my dream or dig deeper into my soul and find the courage to keep going. I realized that I couldn't stop the pain; I couldn't stop the snot from running down my face; but I could stop the courage from leaving my heart!

As everyone stood over me to see if I was still alive, I jumped to my feet and screamed as loud as I could, "Let's play some football!" At first people were shocked. Then, everybody started laughing and saying that I was crazy. My friends have teased me about that moment for years.

After that, the game continued and went right down to the final play. I would like to say that we won that day, but we didn't. When the game ended, the Central fans stormed the field, cheering for their heroes. My teammates and I silently and painfully made our way to the bus for the long ride home. Nobody spoke, nobody smiled. We had lost, we weren't number one; we were number two. As we drove home thoughts of what I should have done differently filled my mind. If only I had given a little more effort. If only I had cut outside instead of inside. If only… Then reality hit me! I would never be able to go back to bring about different results. I'll never forget that day or how miserable I felt when my dream of winning a championship was crushed.

Team Huddle #4
Questions and Answers!

1. Name someone who will or can be instrumental in helping you accomplish your dreams.

2. Have you ever had any major losses in your life?

3. What positive things have you learned from those losses?

CHAPTER 5
High School Hero... To High School Zero

Becoming Focused

The summer before I entered high school was a season of deep thought. During that time, I gathered copies of old Sports Illustrated magazines and began cutting out pictures of the best running backs and championship teams. With every picture I put up on my wall, I could feel my vision growing and my direction becoming clearer. This was the time in my life when I became poetic. Of course nobody knew this because all my poems were written to myself. I wrote poems concerning my dreams and placed them all over my room. My room became a hall of motivation. Every morning when I got up there it was my vision, my destiny. I knew where I was headed in life.

In June of that year, I purchased an old weight set and started lifting weights. At the end of the last school year, there was a lot of talk of me playing varsity football in my first year and I wanted to be ready—just in case. Every day, I spent time in my room lifting weights and looking at the pictures on my wall for motivation.

The best part of my summer routine happened every Saturday morning when my buddies and I would go down to the local Big Boy restaurant and devour their all-you-can-eat breakfast buffet. I put on a lot of muscle mass that summer and nearly put the restaurant out of business! My friends and I spent countless days talking about winning a state championship and wearing a championship ring. After all, we were heading to Arthur Hill High School, one of the top football schools in the State!

When it came to football, Arthur Hill High School was a powerhouse! Loaded with great talent and coaches, we expected to be in the state playoffs every year. Anything less would be a failure. Our high school had the distinction of several undefeated seasons and even one year when our opponents never scored one point against us! The head coach was Coach Jim Eurick. He was a very calm man who could turn into a monster if he had to…but only if he had to. Coach Eurick's football program and staff commanded so much respect that they had very few serious problems with the players. All of us knew that we were lucky to be playing for Arthur Hill, and we didn't take that lightly. Coach Eurick was known to kick his star players off the team if they violated rules and still end up winning big on Friday nights. You wanted to play for Arthur Hill because it was an honor. Coach

Eurick didn't really look like what I thought a coach would look like. Instead, he looked and coached more like a concerned parent. Before I finished my playing days at Arthur Hill, coach would be instrumental in helping me take the next big step toward my dream.

August finally rolled around and football camp started. I could tell the coaches liked what they saw physically, but more importantly they loved my attitude. I wasn't afraid of hard work, and I loved to win. The coaches were also impressed by my speed, so they had me race against their top two players. I didn't do too bad that day. I beat one guy convincingly and barely lost to one guy. By the time the season started, the coaches decided to start me off on Junior Varsity for a few games and then move me up to varsity after I had some experience. I was somewhat disappointed by their decision, but it added fuel to my fire. From that point on, I played to win and to get moved up to varsity as quickly as possible.

JV Football

In some ways playing at the JV level was good for me, because I was able to build an incredible amount of self-confidence. Our JV team was a nightmare waiting to happen to our opponents. We were bigger, stronger, and faster than anyone else in our league. Five or six of us could have easily made the varsity team at other schools, but considering the fact that we were at Arthur Hill, we had to wait our chance to play varsity. As far as our JV team was concerned, there wasn't an offense that could get by us, or a defense that could stop us. Even if the other team's defense was in the right place at the right time, we still would overpower them. We were like men among boys. That year, it was easy to rack up three hundred yards of offense in each game. Due to the great team that I played on, I was able to run for a lot of yards and score quite a few touchdowns as well.

By midway through the season, I was surprised that I heard nothing from the varsity coaching staff. I made up my mind that the next game I would do something significant so they would have to put me on varsity before the season was over. It was game day, and I was planning to have the game of my life. I mentally said my good-byes to my JV buddies because I had plans that this would be my last JV game. I was sure that I was going to score at least twelve touchdowns in that game, despite the fact that I was wearing a second hand pair of cleats that my buddy Willie had given me. I couldn't quite afford a pair. The only problem with this was that Willie wore a size 13 shoe, and I wore a 10 ½. Upon reflection, this must have looked funny to have a five foot-nine inch player running around with very big feet. When I first started running in those shoes, I would be in open field with nobody within ten yards of me to make a tackle only to abruptly trip over the extra 2-3 inches of my shoe. The coaches thought that I was strange, but the truth was my shoes were just too big. I finally got smart and I would wrap tape around the top of the shoe so that my feet wouldn't slip around so much.

The game started as I had hoped it would. My offensive linemen were opening massive holes in the defense for me to run through. By the end of the first quarter I had scored three touchdowns and was well on my way to score twelve by the game's end. Just after the second quarter started I ran up the right sideline for a 99 yard score. Then, we stopped the opposing team and got the ball back. Three plays later I scored again. The second quarter was coming to an end and it looked like I wasn't going to have the chance to score a sixth touch down before half time. Suddenly, one of our guys caused a fumble and we recovered the ball. Fortunately, or at least it seemed like it at the time, the coach called my play. I got the ball, ran behind some great blocks by my teammates and made a mad dash to the end zone. Just as I was crossing the goal line, a player from the other team fell on my ankle. I landed in the end zone and two powerful feelings came over me. The first feeling was that of joy because I was half way to my goal of scoring twelve touchdowns. The second feeling was that of pain. Real intense pain! For the first time in my life I had been injured. At first I thought I was dying, but the coaches let me know that wasn't the case. It turned out that I had a badly sprained ankle and wouldn't be able to finish the game. I was devastated! Both because the game was such fun, but also because I wouldn't be able to grab the varsity coaches' attention the way that I had hoped to…or so I thought. After the game was over, I found out that the varsity coaches had actually been planning to move me up to varsity after that night's game regardless of how well I played. However, because of the injury, they said that it would probably be best to stay on the JV team until I was completely healed. I wanted to cry right there, but I quickly pulled myself together and regained my I-will-not-be-denied attitude.

That night I did break some records, but I didn't exactly get what I wanted. I ended up missing two games due to the injury. We eventually finished the season undefeated; yet there were no championship accolades given in JV football. My teammates and I were satisfied with what we had accomplished together that season.

Varsity Football

At the end of the regular season the varsity coaches finally pulled me and some of my JV buddies up to varsity. This happened just in time to help them make a run for the state championship. The coach made it very clear that he wasn't pulling me up to varsity to watch. He planned on playing me and expected big things. I was so excited I don't think I slept for days. I was playing for Arthur Hill's varsity football team! I felt like I was sitting on top of the world.

From the very first day of practice in preparing for the state playoffs, the coach got me involved with the first string offense. I was actually going to get a chance to play in the upcoming state playoff game. As great as it was to be on the first string offense, there were some bad parts as well. One was that I had to scrimmage against our first string defense. I felt like I was in the land of giants! They pounded me, flipped me, twisted me and after every hit Coach Eurick would just look with a smile on his face and say, "Welcome to varsity football."

By the time the first playoff game started I was really ready to play. I knew that it couldn't be any tougher than practicing against my varsity teammates! As it turned out, we played a worthy opponent, but we prevailed. For me, the highlight of the night was being able to contribute to our win by running a thirty-yard screen pass in for a touchdown. We moved on to the semi-finals the next week, but this time we were beaten by a better team that eventually went on to win the state championship that year.

Losing My Focus

As my high school years went by, I learned a lot about how

people think. Some of what I learned was good and some of it was a real shock. It did not take me long to discover that as long as I used my talents and abilities to make my school look good, people liked me. My classmates and even some of my teachers wanted to be around a winner, someone that they thought would accomplish big things in life. I remember after every game that we won, there was a particular gentleman standing near the exit to congratulate me and tell me that I was the greatest thing since sliced bread. I was certain that he was truly a committed fan who liked me for who I was. Man, was I ever wrong! I learned this after a game against one of our rival schools. In this game, I had played rather poorly, but still had tried my hardest. As I exited the field he was there waiting for me. When I saw him I felt better that at least our fans still supported us even when we lost. I just expected him to say something encouraging like, "You'll get them next year." But he didn't. He looked me straight in the eyes and with a look of disgust, shook his head, snarled something and walked away. I remember how bad that hurt me. Probably because I had learned to trust this gentleman. Sadly, that was the day that I realized that most people only like winners. Losers didn't rate even some basic courtesy, let alone any encouragement. That day I didn't win. That day, I was alone and I hated it. That was the beginning of a very dark and confusing time for me. I found myself beginning to play for the people and their praises. All of a sudden there seemed to be nothing more gratifying than the roar of the crowd as I ran up the sideline and did my back flip in the end zone. Their applause said they liked me; they accepted me; it drew their attention and affections towards me. On those nights when I didn't make it to the end zone, the crowd was silent. Without knowing it, we had built a relationship on conditional love. If I won I was rewarded and if I lost I was shunned.

By the time I reached my senior year, I was hopelessly lost in the cycle of performance, acceptance and rejection that the game of football taught me. Although I played for a great school and a great coach, we never managed to bring home a state championship. Amazingly, in the eyes of many, my team was a failure even though we lost few games. This was hard to take. Even harder to take was the fact that although I was a star athlete in three different sports, I had no peace inside. By this time, I was receiving letters from colleges all over the nation to play football, but I had no joy in my life. To the people around me, it looked like I was living the American high school dream, but to me it had become a nightmare for many reasons. My accomplishments brought with them more than just attention from colleges. They also brought lots of fans who were willing to do almost anything for my own acceptance of them. Looking back, this could have been a wonderful opportunity for a young man who truly cared about others more than himself. It could have been a time when I encouraged and truly loved others like a brother, especially the young ladies in my high school.

Unfortunately, this is not how I used the precious time and opportunities that athletic fame brought me. Sadly, I began to take advantage of others and use my popularity as a means to get whatever I wanted, regardless of who it hurt. The way that I treated my female classmates is a source of great pain for me today. I received attention from many young ladies who wanted to go out with me at this time in my life. This caused my ego to grow to huge proportions. And in my own selfishness, I did not show the respect that these young ladies deserved. A date with me soon came to mean one basic thing—sex.
I have since learned that sex is something that is very wonderful in the context of marriage, but at the time it seemed like fun. On Monday mornings at school, I sometimes bragged about my sexual conquests that happened over the weekend. This kind of activity gave my self-esteem a real boost and at the time seemed like fun. I hurt many young women. Some of them were shattered and their sense of value was destroyed. They knew that they had been used. And I knew that I was a controller, manipulator, and a user. Words cannot express my remorse for the things I did back in those days.

At times, I was dating two and three girls at the same time. This brought out another aspect of my personality that I never knew that I had—lying. As I tried to juggle my relationships with the different girls, I got to the point that I really did not know when I was lying or telling the truth. There were times in these relationships that arguments ended in verbal and sadly physical abuse by both parties.

What was so hard to understand was that my whole life I hated my own father because of the type of man he was. He was a selfish user, an abuser, and a man who left others worse for having

43

met him. I vowed that I would grow up to be a better man than he was. Yet here I was, doing the same things that he had done.

In a rare moment of honest reflection, I realized that I was selfish and out of control. I lived only for the applause of others and to satisfy my own selfish desires. Towards the end of my senior year I hated myself, who I was, what I did, who I did it for and even the very talent that I possessed. Soon, that same hate that I had toward my father for so many years was staring back at me when I saw myself in the mirror.

When Dying Seems Like The Only Way Out

My lifestyle left me empty and soon I went on a deep soul search for truth, purpose and direction. Once in a while, I even mumbled a few prayers to a God that I doubted even existed. The condition of my life left me in deep despair. For three months after every sporting event and every party I went home, sat in the dark and cried like a baby. There was no crowd cheering. There was just me, the dark silence of my room, and hopefully a God that would hear a young man's cry. This was the pattern of my life for three months as I bounced between two different worlds. During the day I would go out partying and enjoying the temporary pleasures of the abusive relationships. At night, I would come home and literally begged God to change me. There in the dark, I poured out my deepest wounds to him and, at times I screamed "If you're out there, make yourself real to me!"

For months there was nothing but silence from Heaven as my prayers seemed to echo off the ceiling in my room. Little did I know that the answer would soon arrive, if I could only wait that long. But patience was not something that I was good at in those days and rather than wait for a divine answer to my questions I made up my own answer, an answer born out of despair. I came to the conclusion that I would take my own life. At that point, death seemed like the only way out. Looking back, I realize that I should have shared my feelings with someone older and wiser than I was. My mom, my coach, a counselor at school or even some of the older uncles in my family, but I didn't. I guess that I did not want them to think I was crazy, or immature, or that I could not handle things. I now know that the combination of fear and pride could have cost me the most precious gift that God gives us –life.

Incredibly, I got up one morning and decided that today was the day that I would die. I dressed and went to school for only one reason, to see my two buddies Willie and Eric for the last time. I remember how anxious I was that whole day. I just wanted to go home and end it all. In a matter of hours, I would be finished with all this mess called life. Or so I thought.

The last bell rang marking the end of the school day and I was soon headed out the door. I decided I would look for a ride home so that I could get there faster. As I reached the parking lot, I saw a familiar face of one of my football teammates by the name of Jeff. I basically told him that I needed to get home in a hurry and demanded that he take me there. The guy looked at me with the biggest smile on his face and replied, "Yeah, I'll give you a ride home!"

Jeff and I had played on the same football team for the past three years and up to that time I had only talked to him once before. That was after he tackled me particularly hard during practice and I told him I was going to rip his head off after practice. To make matters worse, coach Eurick heard my threat to Jeff and sent me off on the treacherous journey of running laps. Coach Eurick telling you to run laps was a player's worse nightmare, because you didn't stop running until he got tired of watching you run. I vowed that day that I would have Jeff's head on a platter, and had just never gotten around to getting the job done. Strangely enough here we were riding in the same car together. It occurred to me that I should keep my vow of hurting Jeff and then go home and kill myself. In my troubled state of mind, it seemed like a great plan.

As we pulled away from the high school, I quietly stared at the track where I had broken so many records. Next, we passed the football field and I envisioned myself racing down the field with the crowd cheering. As the field disappeared from sight, I had a troubling thought. I knew that tomorrow would be here soon, and everyone would wonder why had Brian Pruitt done it? Why did he take his life? For a moment I thought if anyone would really miss me. Quickly, I concluded that they would simply find someone else to cheer for when they won, or ignore when they lost so what did it matter?

The Solution

I was jarred from my deep thoughts as Jeff turned on some kind of rock music. I was further shaken when he turned the radio volume down and asked me a strange question. He asked if I knew that Jesus Christ loved me and had a plan for my life. I was so shocked that I didn't even answer his question. He asked again, "Brian, do you know that Jesus has a plan for your life?" Without thinking, I told Jeff that I wasn't interested in God. Outside I was acting calm, but inside my heart was racing and I could feel anger rising in my belly.

He then said that he needed to stop at a store for his mother, so we did. I figured this talk about God was over and I could get on with the deadly program that was planned. In the seconds that Jeff was gone, I had a brief conversation with myself about God. To me, God must be like my own dad. Big promises but not there when you needed him. Besides, what about the previous three months of prayer with no response? I didn't know it, but that same God had lovingly orchestrated this moment as the answer to all of my heart's cries. I was about to find out how. Jeff soon got back into the car, turned to me and said, "Brian, Jesus loves you." This time I nearly exploded and told him I didn't want anything to do with Jesus. I sputtered that I had been calling out to God for three months and nothing had happened. I bitterly complained that since God didn't want me, I didn't want God!

Jeff took the long way to my house, stalling for any time he could get to tell me of the creator's love for me. By the time we pulled up into my driveway an amazing thing happened. Jeff had convinced me to go to his church youth group with him that night! He said that he was going to pick me up at 6:30 pm sharp. I reasoned that I had nothing to lose and if this Jesus that Jeff talked about so convincingly didn't show up, I would still come home and take my life.

True to his word, Jeff picked me up and drove me to his church. As we pulled up into the church parking lot, I was flooded with conflicting feelings. I was scared, excited, and hopeful all at the same time. Still, there was part of me that knew better than to anticipate that anything good could really happen for me. I secretly felt like this God would be a lot like my earthly dad, all talk and no real action. Nothing could have prepared me for what was about to happen inside that building. An amazing transformation was about to take place in my life!

As soon as I walked into the sanctuary, a peace that I had never known came upon me. My eyes grew big as I saw nearly three hundred teenagers participating in the youth service. While most of the kids there would have died to be in my shoes when it came to sports and popularity, I would have traded every ounce of talent I had for just a touch of the peace I saw in their eyes. Honestly, I don't even remember what the youth pastor talked about that evening. I sat there with tears in my eyes. Each tear carried with it the pain, despair and questions of the past few months. My desire to die was instantly replaced with an intense desire to live and to know the one who had created me. Finally, the pastor requested that all heads be bowed and all eyes closed. He asked if anybody would like to receive Jesus Christ as Lord and Savior. At that point, it was as if I was the only one in the church. I raised my hand. The pastor then challenged us to make our way down to the altar if we were serious about our decision. That was all I needed to hear and I literally ran to front of the church. At that altar, my life was changed forever. Hot tears of repentance ran down my face, and sweet forgiveness that only comes from a loving God melted away the coldness of my heart. That night my destiny was restored. The creator of Heaven and earth touched me in such a profound way that I would never be the same. This new destiny was not comprised of self-centeredness, pride and ego. Instead, its foundation was built on serving others, humility and giving thanks to God for all I was. From that moment on, I would no longer live for myself; instead I would live for God and for the precious people that He had created. I was restored and reborn all in one instant!

That night, as I lay on my bed, it was obvious that God had not only heard my earlier prayers, but also had always been with me. He was the one carrying me through all of the hardships that I endured. He was the one who gave me second, third and forth chances to fulfill my destiny. From that night on, I resolved to never question God's love, presence or direction for my life.

Team Huddle #5
Question and Answers!

1. Have you ever felt like you wanted your life to be over? Why?

2. Do you have someone you can talk to when you're feeling down like a parent, pastor, teacher, coach or friend?

3. What are some right ways to deal with problems? What are some wrong ways and why are they wrong?

CHAPTER 6
Recruited, Rejected and Rewarded

Recruited

After that wonderful night at church, my life began to look up. God began to shape my character into something that I could be proud of, and some big name colleges were recognizing all of my hard work on the football field. I remember how excited I was to get home each day to check the mailbox to find letters from schools such as Michigan, Michigan State, Colorado, and Indiana. It felt good to be recruited, because it told me that people recognized the abilities that God had blessed me with. The best part of the whole process was to show the letters to my mother. She was proud that her little boy was going to play college football. Once again, I felt that I was on top of the world!

Every recruiting letter and special cards that I received was placed away for safe-keeping. I still have them to this day. Each made a statement that my many years of hard work was paying off and that I was expected to go places and do big things.

The most exciting time during the recruiting was when you got to visit the different college campuses. The guys on each football team would wine and dine you in hopes of getting you to choose their school. Everyone including the players, coaches and administrators tried to put their best foot forward hoping to influence your decision. It was comical watching some of the coaches act like they were the father that I never had in order to gain my mother's favor. What made this funny was watching the coaches own players roll their eyes as they heard him give the same line that he had given them in previous years.

Each visit would consist of a tour of the campus, meeting with academic counselors, meeting each team's star players and the various position coaches. Typically, each night would end with me going out on the town with the other guys and then being driven to an expensive hotel to sleep.

One weekend, I had received a call from a coach at Central Michigan University inviting me to visit their campus. At the time, I wasn't too excited about the opportunity since my plans were to attend a much larger university. For some reason, I told the coach that I would come for visit on a particular day. Just hours after I made that commitment, I received a call from representatives of Michigan State University, which was very exciting! Unfortunately, they wanted me to come down for a visit on the very same day that I had committed to Central

Michigan University. Rather than just saying that I had a previous engagement, I told the Michigan State people that I would be there for the recruiting visit. This meant that I had to find a way to be in two places at one time or else I needed to cancel my appointment with CMU.

Although my evening at the church had changed a lot about me, there was still a great deal of work to be done with my character. I confess that I took what seemed like the easy way out and did the worst possible thing—I lied. After days of thinking up the best lie I could think of, I called the coach at CMU and told him one of the oldest lies in the book. I simply told them that I was sick. What could they do to prove me wrong? They couldn't see me from their school. They would never know that I was going to Lansing, Michigan on that weekend. The coach from Central let me know that he was truly sorry that we couldn't meet that weekend, and that he would like to reschedule for a later date. At that point however, I was quite certain that CMU was not the place for me.

The next day I headed to Michigan State for the recruiting visit thinking that my plan of deceit had worked. My stay on campus was fun, and I got to attend a big football game that day as well. After the game I went into the locker room and met the Spartan's star running back Tico Duckett. The Spartans lost a close game that day due to Tico's fumble. I felt like I was in a very special place as I stood next to some of the players. Their locker room had the smell of musty football equipment and wet turf. The walls were bleeding the school colors, green and white. I felt like such a part of the team that day I was even saddened about the loss.

The following day when I returned home from my Michigan State visit I received a surprising call from the head coach at Central Michigan University. After a brief greeting, he asked me how I enjoyed my visit to Michigan State. I was totally shocked! After a long moment of silence I tried to answer, but I was completely tongue-tied. I knew that I was caught in a lie! Somehow, CMU had learned of my visit to their rival school. The fact that I went was not a problem, however now the coaches there knew that I had lied and showed a lack of character. The conversation ended on a bad note that day. When I got off the phone I was relived that I wouldn't hear from them again, or so I thought.

In the weeks that followed, each of my visits to other schools was very similar. It was as if I became a part of that school, its players and its history in just a few hours. Every locker room had its own distinct smell, color and wall of fame or photographs of famous players. As the recruiting process went along I was sure that I wanted to attend the University of Colorado. Even though I had not taken a visit to the campus I had received many letters from them and I was still hopeful things would work out between us.

Rejected

Only months before high school graduation, everything began to fall apart. My lack of diligence on my class work during the early years of high school was finally catching up with me. Even though I had my life together at this time, my past was coming back to haunt me. My low grade point average caused the colleges that were recruiting me to back off. Schools like Michigan, Michigan State, Indiana and Colorado and many other schools stopped sending letters. They questioned my ability to hit the books and still perform on the field when I got to college. My unwillingness to apply myself early in high school was now closing the door on my own sports career. This was frustrating for more than one reason. One day, I had to run something down to the office for one of my teachers. The halls were silent because all the students were in class. As I passed by my coach's office, out stepped the coach from one of Michigan's two big universities. I got excited because I thought that he was here for his fourth and hopefully final, recruiting visit. I just knew that this was my big break, since I had visited his campus many times. What made this chance encounter especially great is that although the coach didn't know it, he was my final hope. Just when it seemed like my dream would die; here came the man who would put life back into it. I felt a surge of great joy as I recalled the times that he had sat at my house and talked with my mother. With a big smile I said, "Hello coach!"

In my mind's eye, I saw him reaching out his hand for a shake, or even putting his arm around my shoulders as he told me how much he still wanted me to play football for his University. Then I imagined how proud my mom would be when I told her that I had a new football home. I would like to say that this all happened in those next few seconds—but it didn't. This coach from the prestigious college simply walked around me and went on his way. He didn't say hello. He didn't smile. He didn't even look at me. He just walked right by. Was this the same man who promised my mother that he would take care of me while I was in college and teach me all about character? It was the same man, but this time there was no family for him to put on a show in front of. As the sound of his footsteps on the hard floor faded, I stood alone in the cold hallway. I felt hurt, angry, and bitter. My heart sank as my dream faded into nothing. The nation would never get to see what I could do.

Then the starkest of realities hit when I realized that the coach was not my enemy. No, my own lack of diligence was my undoing. I had become my own obstacle. A tear rolled down my face as I watched the curtain close on my dreams. As I turned to head back down the hall I could see a familiar image through my watering eyes. It was Coach Eurick. He knew that I just watched my future go down the drain, so the first thing he did was put his arm around me. Then we went into his office and talked. That day, Coach Eurick acted like a concerned and loving parent. He was there for me that day.

My coach's kindness got me through that day, but I still felt like my life was in a mess. Throughout my high school career, I knew what it felt like to be on top of the world and then suddenly, I knew what it felt like to have the world be on top of me. It seemed like nobody believed in me so there could be no second chances. All I could do was wait and pray that somehow God would give me one more opportunity.

The time between that encounter with the recruiting coach and my high school graduation was like an emotional roller coaster. Finally, I stood with the rest of the class of 1991 as we received our diplomas. I remember standing on that stage with all my buddies Willie, Eric and Jeff. We were proud, sad and excited all at the same time. None of us could predict what was about to happen to rekindle the fire of my dream.

Rewarded

As that summer drew to a close my prayers were finally answered. Miraculously, one school was still willing to give me a chance to prove myself in the books and on the playing field.

Incredibly, Central Michigan University called one last time to see if I had signed with any other school! I couldn't believe that they would even want anything to do with me. After all, I had lied to them, mistreated them, and practically told them I didn't want to go to their school.

The coaches made a proposal to get me to their school. They offered that if I paid my own way the first year and proved myself in the classroom, then they would be willing to reward me with a scholarship for my remaining three years. This was called proposition 48. I did not care what they called it. I jumped at the offer! When I hung up the phone, I sat down on my couch and just cried. Then, I got so excited that I began dancing around the house. My dream was back!

Team Huddle #6
Questions and Answers!

1. Name a few things that are or could become obstacles to your dreams.

2. We can sometimes become an obstacle to our own dreams by failing to do well academically. What type of student are you? What can you do to improve?

3. How do you feel when family, friends, or other people in life reject you?

4. How do you deal with or express those feelings talked about in question #3?

Left: Grandparents Ceola and Luterry Pruitt

Below: My cousin Mike and I playing with Christmas gifts.

Below: Sporting my favorite jacket.

Above: With sister Stephany.

Above: My mother Joyce accompanies me to an awards banquet.

Left: High School Stars:
Brian Pruitt, top right
Eric Harrison, middle left
Willy Rodgers, bottom right

Above: Spending time with
my hero, Lawrence McKinely.

Above: Delicia and I
enjoying our wedding day.

Above:
Playing
baseball
with my
brother
Mike.

Above: The Pruitt Family.

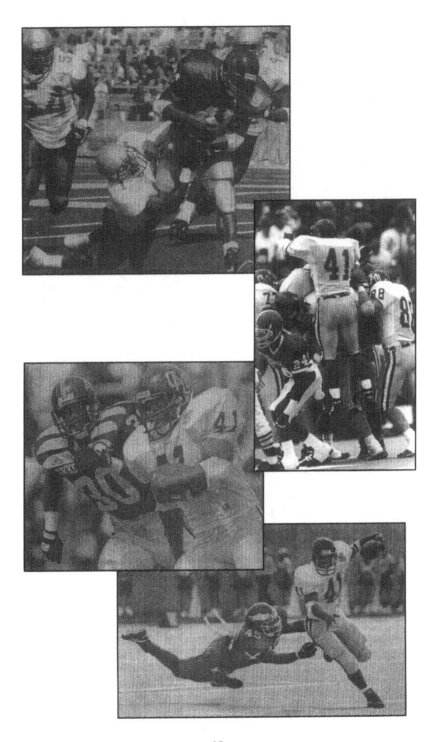

1994 AP All American Team

An opportunity to meet Bob Hope.

CHAPTER 7
The Right Perspective

Ordinary Person

In the summer of 1991, I got a job that would help pay off my first year of school. This allowed me to save just enough money to get started at CMU. During my first year there, I wasn't able to practice with the football team because I was ineligible. This is one of the most painful times that I can remember. I went as far as not going to any of the home football games that year. I knew that it would only drive me crazy to watch other people competing in my game-- football, without being able to play. Instead, I spent my entire first year of college studying to raise my grade point average. For the first time in years schoolwork actually became fun to me again. It was a great feeling to know that I was doing well in school.

Having a year away from football was somewhat of a blessing in disguise. In that year I learned a lot about life and myself. I had plenty of time to focus on my studies. Concerning myself, I learned that there was a lot more to Brian Pruitt than just sports. I didn't need the roar of the crowd to motivate me. Instead, I could be self-motivated. I also learned that I could encourage myself and that I was important. Not because someone cheered for me, or because of what others thought of me. I was important because a loving God that never made any junk created me! That year, I met new friends and learned some amazing things about people. There were actually people who liked me just because I was me. They didn't know Brian Pruitt the athlete, just Brian Pruitt the person. The people I met and the things I learned about life and myself would all become a solid foundation for me in the future.

This was such an amazing time for me. Believe it or not, I had become content not playing football at all. I liked the new me. I loved hanging out at the library doing schoolwork, walking across campus during a fresh snowfall and eating pizza at the local restaurants until I couldn't eat any more. Academically I had focus like never before and was doing great in school.

Climbing a Mountain

In no time, a year had gone by and the "92" summer football camp had begun. It was a scary feeling knowing that I would be getting back on the field. All I can remember was thinking that maybe I didn't want to play football anymore. I knew after a year of not playing that I would be rusty at best. During the previous year I had been so wrapped up in my schoolwork that I never bothered to include daily exercise in my routine. I was in the worst shape of my life!

The dreaded days of August were upon me and football camp was starting. The coach called the first meeting. As the team assembled, I must have looked like a clumsy freshman wandering around in the dark. The coaches looked serious and the players looked mean. Instead of being my dream, the start of my football career at CMU seemed like a nightmare. I was scared!

In mid-August, conditioning and team meetings started. I was most afraid of this time because I knew the coaches would be very disappointed in me. Out of shape, mentally dull when it came to football, I was not what they hoped they were going to see.

Coming into camp I was the sixth string running back. The guys in front of me were sophomores, juniors, and/or seniors who knew the system and to make matters worse, there were some promising freshmen there who were ready to show their stuff.

It turned out that although the coaches were disappointed that I was out of shape, they were impressed with my willingness to work hard to get back in shape. I wasn't sure exactly how I would climb the mountain of other tailbacks that were ahead of me, but I was hopeful because I was improving everyday. One day after practice my running back coach pulled me aside and told me that the coaching staff had made a decision to red shirt me. This meant that I could practice but I would not see any playing time until the next season. Well considering that I had already missed a year of football I was not happy to hear that it would be another whole year before I would touch the playing field again.

I tried to influence the coaches decision by reminding him that I was getting better everyday, but just then I realized something: I wasn't getting better, I was only getting into shape. In order to work on getting better you first have to be in shape. The problem was that while I was trying to get in shape, camp was going on. Right then I knew that if I was going to change the coaches' minds about red shirting me, it wouldn't be by what I said but by what I did. I knew that I would have to perform at a level that would force them to change their minds. Every practice from that point on, I ran harder and further down the field to get myself into shape. Every practice I would make something big happen on the field and show my God-given leadership skills. Slowly, but surely the coach started playing me ahead of other running backs. I was working my way up the mountain.

This Means War

The last thing done during camp is the inner-team scrimmage. Although we were playing against our own team, it felt like we were playing a real game. Traditionally, this scrimmage played a big role in a player moving up or keeping his starting position. I hoped that this scrimmage would convince the coaches that the last thing he wanted to do was red-shirt me. Well, that day as the whistle blew and the scrimmage started, no one played it like a scrimmage. It was a real game, and men were fighting for positions. There were men on that field who grew up just like me dreaming of their destiny on the field. They could also remember their dreams of playing pro football. The fact that we were playing college football put us all one step closer to that dream. I personally knew that if I were to get red- shirted that my career would probably die. Two years without being on the playing field could destroy an athlete. That day the guys I had learned to love over the weeks of practice were no longer my teammates, but they became obstacles in the way of my dream. When men are fighting for their dreams they either gain or lose character. That day, there were men who won on the field, but lost as a person because they deserted their character. They cheated, cut corners, and tried to intentionally injure other players. There were also men who did it right, they won on the field and added to their character by playing fair and square. It was an amazing day filled with hard hits, awesome catches, and stunning runs. After the scrimmage was over the coach called me over and told me that I wouldn't be red-shirted. More than that, I had moved up three spots to the third string position. I was so excited, but I didn't want to stop there. At that point I decided that I would set my goal on being the starting running back for CMU.

Back In The Game

By the time the 1992 season started I was getting just as much playing time as the second-string running back. When he was injured early in the season, I moved into his position for good. As the middle of the season rolled around the coaches noticed that there were some things that the first string running back couldn't do that I could and vice versa. So about mid season we both were considered first string and we split the playing time. Whoever was running the ball well against a team got to keep playing. This was great because it gave both running backs a chance to be the big runner on any given day.

I am excited to say that I did what no one thought I could do, move from sixth string to first string in a matter of months. That season, I ended up leading the team in rushing and scoring. Both were great since I had been out of football for a year and I began the season as the sixth string running back. However, as a team that season, we didn't do very well. We ended up having a 5-6 record, which meant that it was one of CMU'S first losing seasons in years. Although we were disappointed, we were hopeful for the next year.

Going into the 1993 football season everyone was excited to prove that we were better than our previous record showed. We also were all excited to know that even the conference thought we were better than our record showed by picking us to win the championship that year. Although we all came into camp that year with big dreams we didn't have the work ethic needed to bring our dreams into reality. During our summer camp you could see no one put any effort into getting in shape. That year I quickly learned that without good work ethics great athletes become very average!

The early season was like a roller coaster because we were so inconsistent. We managed to win some very tough games but we also lost some that we seemingly should have won. As a team we just didn't have the stamina to make the big plays happen. Fumbled balls, dropped passes, missed tackles, and a lack of discipline equal a lot of finger pointing and blaming of each other. I am sad to say that by mid season we were arguing on the sidelines and we had a lot of team cliques. Everybody on the team thought it was someone else's fault that we couldn't win. Guys would show up for team meetings with black eyes and fat lips that they had received when they got into a fight with their own teammate the night before.

Where's My Confidence?

During this time of struggle, my coach pulled me aside and let me know that he was going to give my starting position to someone else because I wasn't getting the job done. I was crushed! From that point, fumbles, dropped passes and mental mistakes plagued my performance. My confidence began to crumble. I had fallen back into the trap of letting others determine what I thought of myself. If the coaches no longer believed in me, then neither did I. It wasn't long before I also lost my second string position and was sitting on the sidelines watching my buddies play football. For the first time in my life I hated the game of football. I no longer wanted anything to do with it because I lost my love for the game.

An athlete who has his confidence shattered is no good to his team or himself. No one ever knew it, but at that time I began making plans to go back home to Saginaw. It seemed like my way to escape even though I knew my mother would never accept it!

I probably would have carried out my plan if not for an amazing thing that happened one day while I waited on the sidelines during a game. As I looked down the line of athletes standing next to me, I saw that most of them were bigger, faster and stronger than the guys who were starting in front of them. I wondered why these guys weren't contributing to our team, because we could win with them. Following that game, I spent time talking with them until I found my answer-- they were all injured. I don't mean physically injured, but every one of them had their confidence shattered at some point in time. They no longer believed in themselves, and they didn't feel like their teammates or coaches believed in them either. We all had something in common. We were all good athletes who no longer contributed to the success of the team, because we didn't believe that we could. This revelation led me to a sobering conclusion. I realized that in the past, every one of these great athletes had big dreams about being the best. However, somewhere along their journey they had been stripped of their confidence, their dreams, and their destiny.

Then it hit me. I suddenly realized that I was letting a great opportunity to play college football slip away. This is when I made winning the Mid American Conference Championship a priority. Once I set my sights on it, I became hungry for it. Not only did

I want to win the championship, but I also wanted to be the best player in the MAC. I no longer just wanted to be the starting running back. Now, I wanted to make my mark in MAC history.

I went home that night, but I never went to sleep. I stayed up that whole night and I prayed. I asked God to restore my confidence, not in myself, but that I would become confident in what He could do through me. I told God that I wouldn't stop praying until he gave me back what I had lost. That night was long and agonizing. I cried. Sweat poured down my body as I wrestled with the demons that tried to keep me bound in self-doubt and failure. Memories of the critical remarks and finger pointing that had brought me to this point flooded my mind. There in that dark dormitory room, God did a work in my heart. My love, my dreams, and my destiny returned, but something was different. That night, I made a decision to no longer play for my own glory. Instead, I would play for God, my King! My Heavenly Father saved my passion from dying when I couldn't. That night I wanted to make a theme for myself that would always remind me of my vow. That night, the saying "Four for the King" was born. This meant that I would play four quarters of football for God and God alone.

The Power Of Confidence

That week in practice I was a brand new player. I played the game with the joy of a kid again. I hit the holes hard and fast. I broke tackles and made the big play happen. I didn't make mental mistakes. Those things I did do wrong I just said, "I'll get it right the next play". The coach saw that something happened to me and by midweek he placed me at the second string position again. By Saturday, the coach let me know that I was going to get a lot of playing time when we took the field that day!

The game started and as I stood and watched the first string run out to play, I became very anxious. Midway through the first quarter the coach called me up and put me in the game. As I ran onto the field, childhood memories of diving catches and 60-yard dashes to the dirt-piled end zones filled my mind. I knew it was going to be a special day and it was! My team played great, and I had the biggest rushing day of my college career with 200 yards and two touchdowns. The whole time I was playing I just kept thinking, "Four for the King!"

By God's grace, I continued to play with intensity for the remainder of the season. When our final game of the 1993 football season was over, we ended up with another disappointing record of 5-6. The early season losses created too deep of a hole for us to climb out of. While my teammates and I were all happy at our end of the season rally, we certainly didn't feel like champions. That year I watched the MAC championship game on TV and I knew that next year, I had to be there. I heard the roaring of the crowd. I saw the great accomplishments of the players. For one team, the dream had become reality. They were the MAC Champs.

Team Huddle #7
Questions and Answers!

1. It takes hard work to bring a dream to reality. How would you rate your work ethic?

    Great – I go above and beyond what's required.

    Average – I give just enough to get by.

    Poor – I very rarely spend any time improving myself.

2. When you lose your passion or your confidence you have truly lost. How would you rate your:

    Passion for your dream?
    Low 0 1 2 3 4 5 6 7 8 9 10 High

    Confidence to accomplish the dream?
    Low 0 1 2 3 4 5 6 7 8 9 10 High

3. Do you believe in yourself? Why or why not?   What needs to change for you to begin to believe in yourself?

CHAPTER 8
Everything Is Coming Together

All Eyes On The Prize

In the summer of 1994 there was a great sense of urgency in my heart. I was no longer an underclassman. I was a senior; it was my last chance to take a shot at winning the MAC championship. Everyday, thoughts of how I approached past seasons ran through my mind. I was determined to approach my senior year with a different attitude. If we didn't win a championship this year, the opportunity would be lost forever. The guys and I decided that we would meet every morning and workout. This was easy for them since they were all living on campus. At that time, I was living back at home, which was an hour's drive away. This took a lot of commitment to get there every day, but I did it. I knew that I wanted to be a part of what the guys were doing, so I was willing to make the sacrifice.

Everyday that summer we worked hard running, lifting and pushing ourselves to the limit. One day while working out, I pulled the guys aside and explained the theme, "Four for the King." It meant playing four quarters of football for God. I let them know how important my faith was to me and how I nearly gave up my dream. I found out that a lot of these guys were going through the exact same thing I went through. The workout time turned into a group of guys pouring their hearts out to one another. We shared our strengths and weaknesses that day. At the end of the discussion we decided that we all would play, "Four for the King". As we ended our workout that day we made a huddle, and at the count of three we shouted in unison, "Four for the King!"

Love Of My Life and
Love Of The Game

Everything seemed to be going great that summer. I not only found a new passion for the game that I loved, but I also fell in love with my future wife. While in college, I made a personal commitment to myself that I wouldn't date for three years. I just felt like I needed the time alone to focus on my goals of graduating and playing football. After three years of not dating I finally met this tall beautiful, bright-eyed girl by the name of Delicia. Not only did she look good, she also was a great person. Delicia was a student at the University of Michigan who had aspirations of becoming a Doctor. We found out that we had a lot in common. We both seemed to be very goal oriented. Delicia and I were a hit from the start. The thing that I enjoyed most about my relationship with Delicia was that we never tried to become an obstacle to each other's dreams; instead we wanted to help each other accomplish them. The new love of my life seemed to fit right in with my plans. She was beautiful and focused. As time went on, I knew and my mother made sure that she told me that I would be a fool to let Delicia get away. At that point I made plans to put on the "Old Pruitt Charm," and I proposed to Delicia. Thank God she said, "Yes." Things couldn't have been better for me. I had found the love of my life and developed a new passion for winning.

A Turning Point

It had been a great summer. Just when it seemed that nothing could go wrong, the entire team was called in for an emergency meeting by our head coach, known as Coach Deromedi. Everyone was concerned, but no one knew what was going on. As we all sat waiting for Coach Deromedi to arrive, we grew anxious. We wondered which guy on the team did something stupid this time. Finally, Coach Deromedi showed up, and he looked very distressed. He closed the door slowly behind him and took a deep agonizing breath. We all sat in total silence eager to hear what was going on. Coach Deromedi stood in front of the team with tears in his eyes that day, announcing he would be resigning from the head coaching position and moving to athletic director. Everyone's mouth fell open and our hearts just sank inside of us. That day the team meeting felt more like a funeral. Coach Deromedi had won more games than any other football Coach in MAC history, now he was leaving with back-to-back losing seasons. This was not the goodbye party any of us wanted to give to him. He was not only an awesome coach, but he was a man of character. I was proud to be associated with his team. We all left the meeting that day feeling like somebody died. The next week they announced the new head coach. We were all glad to know that he would be someone who was already a part of our coaching staff. They named the defensive coordinator, coach Flynn, as the new head coach. The funny thing was that all the guys on the defensive side of the ball kept calling the new coach "Old Stone

Face". I guess he had earned that nickname after countless years of never smiling on the sideline.

A few months after the coaching ordeal was over, the 1994 camp started. On the first day of reporting to camp the coach would always call a team meeting to share team goals. I remember everybody making comments like: "I like this new coach as my position coach, but I'm not sure what type of head coach he'll be." Funny enough I was thinking the same thing, not to mention the strange nick-name of "Old Stone Face". Coach Flynn entered the room and a code of silence followed behind him. The first thing I did was take a look at his face to see if his nickname fit him. It didn't take me long to agree with the rest of the guys as his cold eyes glared from one side of the room to the other. As Coach Flynn cleared his throat we were all a little nervous. He looked like he was going to start yelling at us. Old Stone Face stood up in front of the team and started the meeting by saying, "Were going to win the MAC championship, and whoever doesn't believe that should leave the room now." Keep in mind that it had been three years since our team even had a winning record, and here the new coach was saying that we were going to win the MAC. I'm sure at that point there were probably a dozen guys who wanted to take him up on his offer to leave, but their mamma's would have beat them all the way back to Mt. Pleasant. Personally, I felt that any coach, who had guts to make a bold statement like that, was a coach that I could grow to like even if people did call him Old Stone Face. We had the same dream that was to wear championship rings and wave championship banners at the end of the season. I'll never forget the look in his eyes that day as they seemed to say, "I've waited for this moment all my life!"

Following that meeting in 1994, we trained like champions because we wanted to be champions. We worked hard. We worked as a team. As each individual's confidence increased the team's confidence increased. Having a new coach made us feel like we were getting a chance to start over. Coach Flynn's coaching techniques were great!

When summer camp was over I knew that it was the best effort put forth by the team in the three years that I had been there. On the last day of camp Coach Flynn pulled us together and gave a speech. The Coach went on to challenge us all once again by saying, "Were going to win the MAC championship and whoever doesn't believe that should leave now!" Once again nobody moved a muscle, but this time it wasn't because they were afraid of their mamma's kicking their butts. This time it was because we believed that we could win.

Team Huddle #8
Questions and Answers!

1.   How do you handle change?

2.   What are some short-term goals that will help you obtain your dreams? This will be a road map for you.

CHAPTER 9
A Long Road To Glory

First Game

It was the first game of the season, and we were going to Iowa to play the Hawkeyes in a non-conference match. As always, everyone was excited, because we were playing a Big Ten school. We had a reputation for pulling off big wins against large schools. In the past three seasons, we pulled off two out of three wins against the Big Ten's Michigan State Spartans. Of course, we were always considered the underdog by the media when playing a Big Ten school, because we were a much smaller school. We never thought we were weaker than teams from big name colleges. In fact, going into each game, we had no doubt in our minds that we could leave the stadium with a win.

The Hawkeyes marched on to the field like soldiers dressed in black and gold. Iowa was known for playing mind games in order to subdue their opponents into losing. A great example of this was the visitor's locker room was painted pink. Their belief was that certain colors effected human behavior. So, they painted the visitors locker room pink believing that it would cause the opposing team to become lethargic while playing.

The game started out well and by the end of the first quarter we were playing even with them. During the second quarter the Hawkeyes brought out their second string. Strangely enough their second string seemed to be just as good as their first and we dropped behind in the score. By the time the third quarter started the Hawkeyes seemed to have an entire new group of men on the field. It seemed as if they were pulling people out of the crowd and dressing them to play! I just kept wondering where they were getting all these people! The fourth quarter rolled around and I was sure that Iowa had played at least six different running backs rotating in and out of the line up. The funny thing was it wasn't the first three running backs that ripped us apart, but the last three. It was almost as if they saved their best for last. The game was far out of our reach. The Hawkeyes showed themselves to be the better team. As we headed back towards the dreaded pink locker room the Hawkeye fans added to our grief by taunting us. That day as we left the field the guys and I called a huddle and at the count of three we shouted, "Four For The King!" After this, no one ever said anything about that game even though some of the guys were really down and probably wondered if they were better off playing for themselves. I ended the game with 14 carries for 97 yards and no touchdowns.

Second Game

It was the second game of the season, and we were to face the Running Rebels of UNLV. Since we lost to them the year before and just came off a tough loss to Iowa the newspapers picked us to lose again. What the polls didn't know is that we had long forgotten our loss to Iowa and we were ready to play! We were not about to let the season start slipping away. As we headed out to the field that day, there was a look of determination in our eyes. Coach wanted us to set the tone for the game right away and you could see he was hungry for a win. After we received the kickoff, our coach called a running play. This was great, because this meant I would get the ball. The huddle was set. The quarterback called the play. Our blood was pumping. I ran the ball once and then twice more. As I got to my feet I screamed, "Four For The King!" The tacklers from the other team looked at me as if I was crazy. They had heard lots of things said on the field, but never had they heard the craziness that was coming from my mouth. That day I didn't care what people thought. All I know is that I felt like I was a kid again, playing football with my neighborhood buddies. That day my teammates and I played with a passion for the game. We played for the King. We broke so many records that day that it was incredible. We beat the Running Rebels and we beat them bad. Heading back to the locker room the media swarmed us. They wanted to talk to the winners. What was really neat was that none of the guys took credit for the win; they all attributed the win to one another. I ended the game with 24 carries for 274 yards and 3 touchdowns.

That week as I went out to my mailbox to pick up the local paper, I noticed they had my face on the front page of the sports section. I couldn't believe what my eyes were seeing; the article was entitled, "The Nation's Leading Rusher." I looked to make sure that it was my face underneath the title again and sure enough, it was me. The combined yardage of my first two games made me the early season rushing leader. I wasn't sure how long I would be on top, so I thought I would enjoy my week of being the nation's leading rusher. I immediately made a call home to my mother, because I just had to share the good news with her.

My mother was excited for me but said that she was not surprised at what her baby boy could do. I knew that I had to stay focused because it was possible to end the season being the nation's leading rusher and still not accomplish my goal of being a part of a MAC Championship team.

Third Game

We were going into our third game and our first MAC conference game of the season. The good news is that we were on a high note but for us our goal of winning the MAC Championship was just starting. In this game, we had to send a message to the entire league. Our opponents were the Eastern Michigan Eagles. This was a team that was rebuilding and doing very well at it. For years, when we played Eastern it was a sure win, but not this season. The Eagles had a new coach who had turned their program around and they had beaten us in the last season. I couldn't believe it was the same team wearing those helmets. They were the same men but they definitely had different attitudes. We knew that we had a dog fight on our hands.

This game was different from the UNLV game. The rebels never expected me to hurt them as a runner. But, now that I was the leading rusher in the nation, everyone started paying special attention to me. Now my teammates and I would have to prove how good we were when people keyed in on our running game. The game was tough. I was running the ball hard, but the defense was swarming in on me every play. The good news was that our second string tailback was having a good game as was our quarterback.

We were losing the game late in the fourth quarter, and finally it hit me. If we lose this game the MAC championship is at stake! This thought boosted my level of play up to hyper speed. BAM! My linemen opened up a hole. SMASH! My receivers made some great blocks. ZOOM! I took off for a 55-yard touchdown. Then the kicker came out and put the game away. We walked away with a two-point win that day. It wasn't pretty, but it was a win. I ended the day with 24 carries for 152 yards and 2 touchdowns. We were having a pretty good season up to this point, but we knew not to get comfortable. In years past we would start the season off great and die out during the middle or last part of the season. In order to win the MAC championship we would have to beat every team that stood in the way of our goal. We decided to take it game by game.

Fourth Game

In the fourth game we were to face Kent State. Kent was not the power house of our league, but they always came to play. We knew that if we were not ready to play, they would pull off a big upset on us. They nearly beat us last year and only a game winning interception kept them from doing so. This year we were not planning on giving them the opportunity to even think about winning the game.

Again, because I was having a great season Kent keyed in on me. Thanks to my fullbacks, linemen, and receivers, whether a team keyed in on me or not, I was able to be effective. One thing that teams didn't realize was that just like the midnight sky has many stars, so did our team. We had plenty of offensive weapons. Stop one weapon and we'd use the other ones. That day Kent looked like they were hungry for a win. They only had one problem, so were we. Kent was another obstacle in the way of where we wanted to go, so we removed them. We pulled off another big one before the home crowd that day. We left no question as to who was the best team on the field. I ended the day with 26 carries for 119 yards, but no touchdowns.

Fifth Game

It was the fifth game of the season, and everything was looking good for us. We were making progress toward our team goal of winning the MAC championship. We knew that we were coming into the most important part of the season.

The Ball State Cardinals were the next team on the schedule. Ball State was the defending MAC champion. We knew that this game would say a lot about where we were as a team. Besides, when you're on top everybody wants to beat you. The Cardinals were on top, and we wanted to beat them. Clearly, this would be a tough game, especially considering the fact that in the past three years neither team had ever won by more than seven points!

The whistle blew, and the guys and I were excited to play. This was it. We were going to get our chance to beat last year's

MAC champs. Ball State won the coin toss and decided to kick the ball off. The Chippewas were ready to play, and it showed as one of our guys returned the ball for a 98-yard touchdown. The crowd went crazy! All the Chippewa fans that followed us to Ball State were waving their Chippewa banners. We did it! We set the tone for the rest of the day--so we thought.

That day we found out why Ball State were champs, because they played like champs. Run after run was stopped; pass after pass was deflected. And, they made big play after big play. The Chips were down, and the Cards were up. Late in the third quarter, the Cardinals had managed to gain a three-touchdown lead.

Finally in the late minutes of the fourth quarter we started to make our move. The offense put together two great offensive drives that ended with touchdowns and we fought our way back into the game. Our defense stepped up and made some big plays and got us the ball back. We were marching the ball down the field and it looked like we would score, because the Cards' defense was getting tired. Once again the champion Cardinals found a way to stop us from getting into the end zone. We had one hope left--we were in field goal range. We attempted a field goal, and made it. We were now only losing by seven points. The game was incredible! Both teams' crowd was going crazy! The Cardinals couldn't move the ball on our defense and we got it back. With very little time on the clock our offense had a chance to win the game. We started driving the ball down the field with our quarterback and receivers doing an incredible job. We made it across the fifty-yard line, then to the Ball State 40-yard line, and then to the 20. The coach called a time out. Our blood was pumping. We only had time enough to try one pass play to the end zone.

The offense lined up, and it seemed like everything was in slow motion. As I looked at the Ball State player across from me, all I saw was two men fighting for a childhood dream. One man was fighting to keep what was rightfully his, the MAC championship. The other was fighting for the chance to say he too was a MAC champion. The ball was hiked, and the quarterback scrambled for as long as he possibly could before throwing the ball to the end zone. The receiver and the defender both wrestled in the back of the end zone. The ball disappeared in a crowd of players. The crowd was totally silent for about two seconds, and then an unbearable roar came from Ball State's stands as a defender knocked the ball to the ground. We fought a giant that day, and we lost. We all knew that this loss could possibly send us on the downward spiral that we had seen in years past during this part of the season. I ended the day with 16 carries for 91 yards and no touchdowns. I remember thinking if I could have only made it to the end zone one time we would have won. I took the loss hard, because I felt it was my fault.

One of the greatest competitors that I've ever known was our quarterback. I remember him saying after the loss to Ball State, "We lost today, but it won't happen again, because I'll make sure of it!" Because of the confidence and the fire in his eyes when he made that statement, we knew that he meant what he said. The coach then stood up and gave a speech to a group of very discouraged players. He started off by saying, "This team is now 3-2 overall and 2-1 in our conference. I know the problems that this team has had in winning during the middle of the season, but not this year. This year you can still win the MAC championship, but you can't lose one more game. This year you can win the MAC championship, but you've got to play to the man!" "To the man" was a phrase that we used which simply meant every man had to give 100% every play, every game. We all knew that in our conference that one loss could ruin our chances to be MAC champs; two losses would certainly dismiss us.

Sixth Game

After coming off the hard loss to the Cardinals we had to play our conference rivals, the Western Michigan Broncos. We knew we were getting ourselves into a fight with another conference giant. It was always a tough game when we played the Broncos. To let you know how good they were, this year they were rated the number one team in the MAC. This was a real challenge for us as a team. After playing the 1993 MAC champs and losing, you would rather not play the team picked to win the 1994 championship the following week!

The Broncos came out fighting! We could get nothing going on offense. It was like we were still dazed from the previous week's loss. Before we knew it, the Broncos were up 14-0. The scary part was that we were still in the first quarter.

We managed to keep them from scoring in the second quarter; but you could tell the Broncos had come to Mt. Pleasant to win. We were really struggling as a team and wondered if we could get over the mid season plague that had seemed to haunt us for the past two years. As I walked on the field after a play, one of our guys looked at me and yelled, "Hey Pruitt! Four For The King!" I then remembered that we made a team vow to play four quarters of football for God. I knew right then that we couldn't give up. Just before half time we managed to toss one into the end zone for a touchdown and went in at half time only down by seven points.

At halftime, there was a lot of deep soul searching going on. Some saw this as a sign that we would crumble. Then there were some of us who were willing to fight to be the champions we all grew up dreaming about. I sat there and remembered the feeling that I had the previous week when we lost to Ball State, and I knew that I never wanted to feel that way again. I screamed "Four For The King!" as we ran back onto the field for the second half.

The coach called my play, and I ran for over twenty yards due to some great blocks by my linemen. The coach called my play again, but this time not only was it a good run but something amazing happened. The whole atmosphere of the game changed. I felt like a warrior fighting for my homeland. The coach knew that something had changed. He pulled me aside and said, "We're riding you all the way through this one." Our running game was on full throttle that day. A number of players made big plays. The Broncos couldn't move the ball on our defense at all. We really took it to the Broncos that day. After all the smoke had cleared from our offensive weaponry, we were able to walk away with a 35- 28 win over the Broncos. I finished the day with 34 carries for 145 yards and 3 touchdowns.

Seventh Game

In our seventh game we faced the Akron Zips. Everyone on our team felt that we owed them one after the beating they gave us the previous year. This year we were going to Akron for just one reason, the big pay back. We wanted to take back what the Zips stole from us a year ago--our respect, our dignity, and our Chippewa pride.

Right before we took the field our coach would sometimes tell us all the bad things the other team's coach had said about us. I never knew if he was telling the truth or not. I really didn't care. Incentive is very important and it can be used like fuel. The fact that the game was going to be on television also gave us great incentive to play our hardest.

From the beginning of the game we took control. On offense we pounded the Zips. On defense we smashed the Zips. The Zips had stirred up a hornet's nest. That day we accomplished our goal to get our revenge. We started out fast and finished faster. We put the Zips away quickly. The offensive line, fullbacks, and receivers made great blocks allowing me to rush for 145 yards and 2 touchdowns on 22 carries.

Eighth Game

There we were in the middle of the season winning ball games when we needed to. The eighth game of the season is always important, because it is the last of mid season play. Then you move on to the final part of your season by playing your last three conference opponents.

For the eighth game, we faced the Miami of Ohio Redskins. In the past two seasons that I had been at Central, we had never beaten the Redskins. We entered the stadium very focused that day, ready to play "Four For The king." From past history we knew that we would be in for a rough game. The Redskins wanted nothing more than to ruin our mid-season victory party.

The game started out well for us. We weren't in the habit of waiting for other teams to strike first. We went for the first punch and the knock out. The championship was on the line every time we took the field at this point in the season and we could not afford to lose another game. Knowing this, we took the ball on the opening drive and marched down for a score. It felt like a great day. The Chippewa express was off and rolling.
We kicked the ball off, and in the transition one of our best players got hurt. He was greatly needed if we were going to win. The game continued, as both teams fought like they were on a battlefield.

At half time we went in and came out knowing what we had to do to win. At this point in the game the score was tied. We knew that in order to win the game we would have to persevere. Two or three plays into the first series, I took a hit that put me out for the rest of the game. I went to the sidelines thinking the pain would wear off, but it never did. The team doctor told me that I wouldn't be able to play the rest of the game. It was a close game, and there were still two quarters left to play. If there was going to be a big game, then I wanted to be apart of it.

I always believed that big time players showed up for big time games. No one wanted to win more than me, and I wanted to take it upon myself to see that it was done. At this point you would think things were bad enough, but things got worse. Five other of our starters got injured right before the fourth quarter started. The score of the game was just going back and fourth at this point. I looked on the field and I saw second, third, and fourth string players. I looked back towards the sidelines and there was a lot of confusion on the guys' faces. None of us could believe that this was happening.

It was the final minutes of the fourth quarter, and it wasn't looking good. The Redskins were getting stronger and were up by five points. Their defense was not allowing us to move the ball. It looked like our championship dreams would be dashed on the stones. After a few transitions of the ball from one offense to another, the clock had run down to forty seconds. The coach called a time out and told the quarterback to run the two-minute offense. During this time the coach also gave us a pep talk, reminding them that we had come to win the championship, and we wouldn't settle for less. As the team took the field with forty seconds on the clock, one time out left, the ball on our on twenty-yard line it looked bleak. Our offense was missing most of its starters due to injury and the crowed roared so loudly it felt as if the stadium would come tumbling down. On the side lines my team mates and I started yelling, "Four For The King!" "Four For The King!"

We had to march the ball eighty yards in forty seconds. The ball was hiked; the quarterback dropped back. He couldn't find anybody, so he ran up the field for twelve yards. We ran another pass play, and the quarterback completed a pass that put us over the fifty-yard line. After each play our players would wisely step out of bounce so that the clock would stop. On the third pass play the ball was dropped. The fourth play of the drive, the quarterback had to run for his life as the Redskins blitzed in their linebackers. He managed to elude his tacklers and fall to his knees calling a time out at the Redskins thirty five-yard line. At this point in the game there was nineteen seconds on the clock. We were down by five points, and we were in position to make a play for the end zone. The crowed was going wild as we marched the ball down the field in the last seconds of the game. The sidelines for both teams were in total chaos. Both sidelines were filled with men whose dreams of becoming champions hung in the balance. We lined up to run another play. This one would be a pass to the end zone to see if we could win the game. The ball was hiked. The Redskins were all over our quarterback, but he managed to toss the ball into the end zone. The crowd stood in silence to see who would come down with the ball as men fought for position. The ball bounced around a few times and then landed on the ground. The Redskin fans were ecstatic. The bad news was we didn't complete the pass in the end zone. The good news was we still had four seconds left on the clock, which was just enough time to run one more play. For the last time the quarterback dropped back. The offensive line did a great job blocking, giving him time to sit in the pocket. Our quarterback scrambled waiting for one of his receivers to break free. After about six seconds of running for his life he tossed the ball into the end zone. The entire stadium was on their feet as the ball went into a crowd of defensive players. About four different players jumped for the ball all at the same time. Three of them were Redskins, and one was a Chippewa. Somehow, out of all the players that jumped in the air for the ball our star receiver was able to come down with the ball, landing in the end zone. The team and the crowed came pouring out onto the field. You would have thought that we won the championship that day. Players were crying, hugging, and shouting. We had won the game 32-28.

In the midst of all the celebration I happened to look at the other sideline at the Redskins. The look on their faces where burned into my memory. Their hopes of being MAC champs had been destroyed in forty seconds. They looked like men without purpose or destiny. We had stolen their love for the game. Defeat is ruthless with the human heart. For just a second I felt sorry for the guys on the other sideline, because I knew what losing felt like for two long years. I knew that I never wanted to feel that way again.

Although I got hurt in the first half of the game, I was able to contribute to my teams victory by rushing for 189 yards on 26 carries, scoring 1 touchdown. Our quarterback was my hero that day. I remember him saying when we loss at Ball State, that he would make sure that we wouldn't lose again. He kept his word. We needed him to step up, and he marched us eighty yards down the field in forty seconds. You should have seen the leadership that he displayed that day.

Ninth Game

After a hard game the week before and coming off of a storybook win, we were all excited to play our final three opponents. The next team on our schedule was the Ohio University Bobcats. We knew that we were going into their stadium and that they wouldn't just roll over and lose, especially since our last game was so close. At this point in our season, every game was the championship game. The Bobcats were good enough. But, what made them even better was that we still had some guys hurt from the last game. Those of us who could play injured that week gritted our teeth and gave the team all we had. I was thankful that the doctor released me to play. I never wanted to be on the sidelines again while my team was at war. The Bobcats were in our way of winning the MAC championship, so they had to be removed. One thing about Central Michigan was that we didn't have just one rival team. Every team we played in our conference looked at us as their rival.

We came out sluggish that day. I guess the hard game from the week before and the long bus ride to Ohio hurt us. The Bobcats on the other hand came to play. We fooled around and found ourselves in another dog fight that Saturday. We just couldn't get anything going, and the Bobcats weren't going to let us either. By the time half time came, the Bobcats were winning the game. This was a team who had no hopes of winning the MAC, but that's what made them so dangerous. The Bobcats had nothing to lose, and they wanted to be sure that we wouldn't win the MAC championship either.

The second half wasn't really that much different. The Bobcats were still playing a good game; we were still playing sloppy football. We just kept hanging in there until we could wear the Bobcats down a little bit. Finally in the fourth quarter we turned the game around. We put together two nice drives for touchdowns. Then, our defense kept the Bobcats from scoring the rest of the game. We got out of Ohio that day with a win, but just barely. We won 22-10. However, the score of the game didn't show the difficulty of the game. I ended the day with 38 carries for 183 yards and 2 touchdowns.

Most importantly, our team was now 7-2 overall and 5-1 in our conference. With two games left in the season this made us one of the few teams who were still able to win the championship. The next two games would be crucial.

Tenth Game

It was the tenth game of the season. Coach told us that if we won that day, we would have the opportunity to play for the MAC championship the following week. Our team was excited to learn that we were sitting on the doorstep of all our childhood dreams. One team stood as an obstacle to our destiny, the Toledo Rockets. I remember that whole week telling myself to make sure that I did all that I could to win this game and give our team the chance to play for the championship. If we lost this game, the next week would be nothing but the last game of the season. We just had to win.

As we sat in the locker room before the game, fire burned in our eyes and spirits while listening to the coach's speech. The coach painted a beautiful picture of a team that had struggled over a few years to be what they knew they could be, the champs of the Mid American Conference. We knew that day that we couldn't play another close game with a team as we had the last two games. We had to put the Rockets away right from the start, since it would obviously be a great victory for them if they won. The victory would be made even sweeter for the Rockets knowing that they would have ruined our chances to win the championship.

The game started and our offense took the field first. We ran our first play and wham! Right off the bat it was clear that the Chippewas had come to win. On the next down I got the play call. I broke through the line, came face to face with a linebacker and went into my spin move. The linebacker missed me, and I took off for a 55 yard score. I went into the end zone. As I entered the end zone I knew that in order to ensure my team victory I would have to visit the end zone often that day. I made up my mind that it would be a day that I would play for the King and see a little boy's chances of becoming a champion come true.

That day, Toledo wasn't just playing against football players; instead they were playing against the childhood dreams of men who refused to lose. Those childhood dreams had outlasted years of defeat, discouragement and pain. Now that they were on the verge of being fulfilled, nothing in the world could stop them. On that day I scored and then I scored again. By the time the third quarter was ending, we were up by two or three touchdowns and well in control of the game. But, I felt like I had to keep running, so I scored again. Finally to make sure the game was out of reach, I took it in for another score. By the time the game had ended, I had run for a total of 434 multipurpose yards and scored five touchdowns. This turned out to be more yards than any other running back had rushed for in one game in all of Division 1A football in 1994. That day I also broke the MAC single season rushing record. All of this was made possible by my teammates who were just as determined as I was to get to the championship game. We won the game 45-27. My teammates and I had just played one of the most awesome four quarters of football ever seen in MAC history. We did it by playing four quarters of football for the King. See you at the championship game!

Team Huddle #9
Questions and Answers!

1. On our way to the championship game we lost our first game of the season, but we didn't give up. How do you handle defeat?

2. What role does team work from team mates, family or friends play in you reaching your goals?

CHAPTER 10
I've Waited For This Moment My Whole Life

The Championship

It was the week of the championship game, and all I can remember was all the press that surrounded the game. Members of the media were everywhere and there was no escape. During that week, I remembered all the times that I had played in championship games and what it felt like when I won or lost those games. I remembered the joy of victory and the pain of defeat. I cherished the moments of victory, and I grew sick to my stomach when I thought about my moments of defeat. I greatly wished that I could go back and change the outcomes of past games, but I couldn't. Memories of those losses brought with them feelings of total helplessness and thoughts of "I wish I could" and "if only." All I knew was that I didn't want to leave my college career carrying thoughts that would haunt me for the rest of my life. Saturday came quickly and I was glad, because I was tired of thinking and dreaming of being MAC champions. I just wanted to make it happen.

For the championship game we would be playing the Bowling Green Falcons. In the three years that I had played for Central, Bowling Green was always our toughest opponent. For years there had been bad blood between us. In the late eighties and early nineties the Falcons had won the MAC championship quite often. They were a power house in our conference, but they always had problems beating us. For some reason the Chips just always seemed to pull it together when playing in big games against the Falcons. This season, the Falcons would also be playing to claim the title of MAC championship. The stakes were high for this game. It was literally all or nothing.

Right before the game started the Coach called us all to the middle of the Falcon's field and ended the season just as we had started it, with our goal. As we stood there, the Coach pointed towards all the championship banners that the Falcons had hanging from their stadium. We were impressed with the many consecutive years that the Falcons had proven to be the best in our conference. Coach then went on to say that the 1994 MAC championship banner would not be found in Bowling Green, because it would be back at home hanging in the Central Michigan football stadium. Then the Coach ended his speech by saying, "We are going to win the MAC championship and whoever does not believe me can leave now!" Once again no one left the field. Because our Coach believed in us so much, we now believed in ourselves. The guys and I called a huddle, and at the count of three we shouted, "Four for the king!"

When the game started we were ready. The Falcons received the ball first, drove the ball down the field, and scored. We knew that we had to strike back quickly. During our first offensive drive on the third play of the game, we ran an option play. The guys ran the play to perfection. The quarterback pitched the ball to me at the last second, which fooled the defense. I caught the pitch, ran off a great block by my receiver, and took off for 50 yards for a touchdown. The game was tied. The game went back and forth. The Falcons were looking good as usual, but so were we. Both defensive teams were doing a great job making it hard for the other team to score touchdowns. In fact, each time a team made a field goal it would put them in the lead. In the second quarter our defense came up big. One of our linebackers made an interception and took it all the way back for a touchdown.

Our defense had become pretty good at making interceptions. Quarter after quarter our defense would come up with an interception that would stop the Falcons from moving the football down the field. The game was an all out battle. Players on both sides of the ball seemed to no longer be playing the game, but instead it was as if our destinies wore helmets and played that day. Everyone on the field played to their fullest potential.

We went into half time with a small lead. As we sat in the locker room one of the guys stood and shouted, "Two more quarters to go before we can say that we're the champs!" The whole time we were in the locker room I just kept saying to myself, "Four For The King." It seemed like the game was going by so quickly. I really wanted time to slow down so that I could just enjoy the moment. Because I was a senior, I knew that this would be the last time that I would have the chance to play with some of the greatest guys in the world. However, time wasn't stopping for me. The Coach blew the whistle and halftime was over.

When the falcons came back out of the locker room after halftime, they were pumped up. They immediately took control of the game and scored. After that, their defense came out and stopped our offense. Then, their offense went on another march down the field. However, as they ran a pass play to the end zone, our free safety intercepted the ball. Our defense was coming up big! When we got the ball back I was running what was supposed to be a five-yard pass route. As I was running my route it was as if God told me to go into our end zone so that when the ball was tipped I could catch it for a touchdown. Strangely enough I followed my heart, knowing that if this didn't work out the Coach would be all over me for changing a five-yard route into a 35 yard route. Sure enough, the quarterback threw the ball to the end zone. Our receiver and the defensive player went up and fought for the ball. The ball bounced off the crowd of people surrounding it and into my hands as I fell into the end zone. We were going wild! As my teammates dove on me I lay in the end zone in amazement asking, "God, was that you?" This touchdown put us in the lead going into the fourth quarter.

The Falcons were not out of it yet. In the middle of the fourth quarter, they drove the ball down the field and scored. This gave them the lead. The whole game was a battle as each team had control of the lead several different times. We received the kickoff, and our offense was in and out in three plays. Since we were on our own thirty-yard line, we were all set to punt the ball. It was fourth and twelve, late in the fourth quarter and we were losing. This seemed like the right time to punt the ball, so we all thought. The only person who happened to think differently was our punter. When the ball was hiked, he decided to fake the punt without anyone, not even the Coach, knowing it. The whole Falcon team bought the fake right along with us. The punter started rumbling down the field, and I do mean rumbling. This guy couldn't run at all which is why he was a kicker. During this play, I was standing right next to the Coach as we all started screaming. None of us could believe what our eyes were seeing. All I remember is hearing the Coach saying, "I'm going to kill that kid!"

Suddenly, our screams turned into shouts of encouragement. We noticed that he had not only picked up the first down but he was actually making his way down the field. We all started yelling, "Go! Go!" Amazingly, he stumbled into a move and faked out a tackler. It seemed like we were watching him run forever, that's how slow he was running. Eventually he made it all the way into the end zone for a score. The crowd was going crazy; the guys on our team who had seen the run were laughing. Players from both teams were wondering what happened.

After our punter had given us the lead with his incredibly courageous run, the Falcons managed to pull themselves together. They once again made some big plays and took the lead by scoring another touchdown. Neither team would quit. We were like warriors fighting to the death. With less than four minutes on the clock, we got the ball back. The quarterback called the huddle and said, "That's it." "The whole season comes down to this drive right here!" "Let's do it!" We took the ball down the field. We weren't going to be stopped. We completely wore the Flacons defense down with an eighty-yard drive. Our offense grew stronger every play, while the Falcons seemed to be dying out quickly. We marched the ball down the field as if destiny stood in the end zone calling our names. With under two minutes left in the game, we could taste victory.

With fifty-five seconds left to go in the game we had finally marched the ball down to Bowling Green's five-yard line. All of the fans in the stadium were on their feet screaming at the top of their lungs. To my right there was a river of fans dressed in orange and white cheering for the hometown team, the Bowling Green Falcons. The Falcons fans were calling us names I dare not repeat. To my right things were looking and sounding a lot better, a sea of maroon and gold. The faithful fans of the Central Michigan Chippewas. Both teams were waiting to see who would get to charge the field and chant "We're number one!" In front of me lay my dreams, the MAC Championship. After two years of losing seasons at Central, we were five yards and fifty seconds away from being the MAC champs.

The quarterback called the huddle as he tried to dislodge a pile of grass and mud that had gotten wedged between his helmet and his facemask during the previous play. While standing in the huddle I took a look around and every man had eyes as big as silver dollars. This was not the look of fear but the look of hunger. We had been starved of winning for two long seasons. Now, we were hungry for a win and to us that end zone represented a buffet.

The quarterback called the play and to no one's surprise I would be receiving the ball. At this point in the season I was competing for the title of the nation's leading rusher. Suddenly one of my linemen began to motivate himself by growling like a mad dog. I thought that he was having a heart attack! Steam was rising from his head like a locomotive train. He quickly turned towards me and through his tightly clenched teeth snarled, "Follow me to the end zone, Pruitt!" Clenching his fist, he promised that he would trample the guy across the line from him. In return I said, " I'll meet you in the end zone!" The quarterback demanded that the ball be hiked on three. Then he yelled, "Ready!" In response to him we yelled, "Break!"

Both teams approach the line of scrimmage staring into the eyes of the enemy. The crowd went into an uproar. Off in the distance I could hear a group of guys on our sideline chanting, "Four for the King!" Bowling Green's defensive players were slapping each other across the helmet and boasting that nobody was going to get into their end zone. The quarterback yelled, "Down!" Our offense slowly and painfully went down into position. The game had taken its toll on us. "Hut one!" I looked across the line of scrimmage and both linebackers were staring me straight in the eyes. Today, they weren't just men but they were obstacles in the way of my dreams. Time stood still at that moment. I began to think about how I felt when I played for the North Vikings against the Central Cougars for the city championship. We lost that day and the Cougar fans charged the field. I remember getting on the bus a loser and coming to the realization that I couldn't play the game over. In my high school career I always dreamed about winning the state championship game in the Pontiac Silver Dome, and wearing the state championship ring, but it never happened. It seemed as if I was always coming up short. I quickly told myself that this time I'm getting on the bus as a winner! This time I'm playing for the championship, and I'm going to wear the ring!

The quarterback yelled, "Hut two!" Thoughts of the past few losing seasons began running through my mind. Finally I would get the chance to vent my frustrations! I didn't want to play my last college game and leave a loser. If this would be my last time wearing the maroon and gold and playing with great men, then I wanted to go out a winner.

The noise from the crowd was deafening by this point. Faintly you could hear the quarterback say, "Hut three!" The ball was hiked. The linemen on both sides of the ball smashed helmets so hard it sounded like a plane crash. Mud was shooting up into the sky from cleats that were digging deep into the ground. Players began to grunt and scream in hopes of finding the strength to give one hundred percent in what could be the last play of their collegiate careers.

As the quarterback sprinted towards me for the handoff, a defensive lineman slipped through our offensive line. Just as the defender smashed into our quarterback, he somehow managed to hand the ball off to me. Instinctively, I side stepped another defensive linemen that had crashed through our blockers. Suddenly, I had been launched like a rocket whose destination was the moon. I could see it, the goal line. I could hear it, my destiny calling me into the end zone. I could feel it, footsteps away from victory. As I came near the goal line, at what seemed to be the speed of light, only one last defender remained. Viscously, he came towards me like a lion protecting his territory. But as swift as a gazelle I slipped through his arms and crossed the goal line… TOUCHDOWN! We were MAC Champions!!!

I ended the day with 29 carries for 144 yards and 3 touchdowns. More importantly I ended the day with the realization of my childhood dream. The crowd rushed out, and we celebrated right there in the middle of the Falcon's field. The guys and I stood enjoying the moment as we cried. We won the MAC. Boy, did it feel good to be on top! We finally made it back to the locker room and called a huddle. We started the season shouting, "Four For The King!" And now, we ended our season shouting, "Four For The King!" By this time I was convinced that God was a Chippewa fan.

After a week of living the champion's lifestyle, my Coach pulled me into his office and told me that I had been selected as a First Team AP All-American. I was very excited to be selected because this was not only a compliment to me as a player but was also a great compliment to all of my teammates who made everything possible. I also found out how the race for the nation's leading rusher ended. I finished in second place with 1, 890 yards rushing, 2,299 multipurpose yards, and 22 touchdowns.

CHAPTER 11
Dreams Do Come True!

The Aftermath

The season had come to an end and we were the MAC Champs. I had just gotten back from spending an exciting time in Los Angeles on the Bob Hope show. It was truly a special time as I reflected on finishing the season as the nation's second leading rusher, second in all purpose yards and scoring touchdowns. Also, the honor of being selected one of three AP All- American running backs in the country was incredible!

One day as I was going through some fan mail I noticed someone had sent me a Sports Illustrated Magazine. As I opened it I notice a letter taped to the cover that told me to look on a particular page. As I turned to the page suggested I ended up reading about a guy named Brian Pruitt that had been named the Sports Illustrated Player of the Month! They even had a picture of me. I couldn't believe what I was seeing.

I started reading other letters from fans. This was different; since I had not read a news article or any fan mail all season because I wanted to stay focused. So I just jammed any fan mail or news articles that people would send me in the corner of my room until the end of the season. I was very surprised that people were sending me fan mail! At the same time I was very grateful to hear their words of encouragement. I began to notice that some of the letters were making references of seeing me on ESPN. That shocked me greatly! I didn't have Cable TV at the house that I was living at so I had never watched ESPN.

The joy and surprises of that wonderful season never seemed to stop. After the Bob Hope show, I received an invitation to come to Ohio as one of the candidates for the Mid American Conference's Offensive Player of the Year award and the MAC Most Valuable Player award. This was an exciting time for my family and me!

The drive to Ohio was a great time for my mother and I to spend some time together. My biggest fan was always my mother. I could tell that she was proud to see what her little boy had become, not a great athlete but a very respectable young man. She knew the pitfalls of the inner city, the despair of growing up fatherless and the previous depths of my anger. We had made it through! Her baby boy was now a man and her job was done and done well. There was no one more excited about the things that I had accomplished on the field and no one prouder that Brian

Pruitt would be graduating from College. Not only was I going to graduate, I was going to graduate having made the Dean's List a number of times during my collegiate career.

When we finally reached Ohio and the awards ceremony, I was quite nervous. There I was standing before the most important men and women in the MAC. I had already made up my mind that I wasn't going to be stressed out about winning any awards. I knew that the competition between the candidates would be great and that we all represented the best of the Mid American Conference. All the candidates were called to the stage area in procession. As each candidate's name was called a highlight film of their greatest plays was shown on a big screen. It almost made you feel like a movie star. The crowd would stand to their feet and applaud. After we all had made it up to the stage and listened to the main speaker for the night, the master of ceremonies stood to make the big announcement. The room was filled with great expectation. The speaker said that all of the candidates were worthy of the awards but only one person could leave with the actual trophies. He then took a deep breath and announced, "This years winner of the Mac offensive player of the year award goes to... Brian Pruitt!" Another goal had been accomplished. As I went to receive the award thoughts of my past filled my mind. I remembered that just a year ago my coach had decided to put me on the bench and the discouragement that I felt sitting on the sidelines. Now I was the MAC Offensive Player of the Year as well as an AP All American. I remembered the little boy who played football with the older guys wanting to be the star of the game. Well, now I had made enough big offensive plays that my conference was honoring me. This time I did it and there were no ditches of dirty water for anyone to knock me into.

As I headed back to my seat my mother and I celebrated with hugs and kisses. The speaker then prepared to announce the winner of the MAC Most Valuable Player Award. I was sure that after winning the Offensive Player award that it would disqualify me for the MVP. All of a sudden people were clapping and thinking that I must have missed something I started clapping for whoever just won the MVP award. I looked up on stage to see who had won but I saw nobody. Suddenly I noticed that everyone was looking at me. I had also been chosen as the MAC MVP!

As I received my award I was asked to share a few words. I

made it very clear that I was very appreciative of the awards but I was just a guy with a dream. My mother was the person who helped to give birth to that dream early in my life. I wanted them to know that back in Saginaw Michigan at a little elementary school in the inner city was a coach who believed in me so much that I refused to quit. I wanted them to know that there were coaches who challenged and gave me the opportunity to go after the dream. I also told them that there was a group of guys in Mt. Pleasant Michigan; now known as the MAC Champs, that made the blocks that allowed me to fulfill the dream. Finally I told them that there was a King that allowed me to live the dream. I played, as I would live, and pointing to the sky I said, "For the King." The crowd stood to their feet and applauded.

Weeks later, I was invited to play in the Hula Bowl, East-West Shrine Bowl and the Blue Gray Bowl. I was stunned by these invitations. I was about to have the opportunity to play in the most prestigious college bowl games in America. Slowly but surely all of my childhood dreams were coming true.

To make the week even better we were scheduled to pick up our championship rings. The entire team was filled with excitement. This championship ring was a physical sign of the heart, courage, and commitment that we had displayed as a team. It would be something for the rest of our lives that would remind us of a place where men of different races and backgrounds came together in unity for one common purpose. For one short moment in time a group of men forgot about themselves and focused on God and a shared dream of winning a championship. As we reflected on all of the great things that had recently happened we found out some deep truths about what really matters. Life wasn't about us; instead it was about the King. When the whistle blew I felt closer to Him than any other time. God was real on the field. Whether we won or lost wasn't the issue. The issue was that we played four quarters of football for the King.

CHAPTER 12
King Mania

People began to call and request that my teammates and I come and speak to large groups of kids. All of a sudden I was traveling two or three times a week to speak at youth events. Everywhere I went I began to share on the theme, "Four for the King." I told the people all that I had accomplished on the field was birthed out of doing everything for God. I stressed the importance of listening to the parents, hard work and persevering. I shared with them the story of a young kid who grew up with a dream but who had faced lots of life's obstacles. Often, it was as if the crowd hung on every word I said. Not because I was a superstar, but because I was speaking to their hurts, struggles and dreams. Some had given up the hopes of accomplishing their dreams due to the frustrating circumstances of life. Although they were young they reminded me of myself. They wanted something that always seemed to be just out of their reach. When they found out that there was a King that was bigger than those circumstances and wanted them to succeed and not fail, their hopes were restored. They began to remember their childhood dreams and were willing to run after them again. I told each group that I spoke to, "Do it and do it for the King!"

Many times after speaking people would come up and confirm what I saw in their eyes and sometimes even in their tears as I was speaking. They would say that they just received a second wind or the courage needed to run a little bit harder towards their goals. They were happy to meet someone who could relate to their struggles and their dreams. These were kids who might not have wanted to be athletes but some wanted to be doctors, lawyers, teachers, and even mothers and fathers.

For the first time in my life I knew how my elementary coach Lawrence felt. He had seen in me what I now saw in them. They were people full of potential that just needed a word of encouragement or someone to believe in them.

It became obvious that the phrase "Four for the King" was not just for football. It was all about life and living life for God, which allows you to live life to it's fullest. After speaking to each crowd I could see that the people were excited not just about a phrase, but a lifestyle. It was so practical they could apply it to everything they did. Remember; no matter what your goal in life is give it one hundred percent --for the King!

Final Thoughts

As I reflect back on all that happened in my life, I see that there are five foundations that helped me achieve success. I want to share them with you here for one reason. So that you can become all that you were created to become!

Foundation Number #1: Dream big

Shoot for the stars and beyond! A wise man once said "how sad to aim at nothing and hit it!" A man without a dream is a man without a dream. Having a dream or something to reach for keeps you focused and gives you motivation for life. Shoot for the stars and even if you miss you still would have least touched the sky. I believe that to live life to it's fullest that one needs a dream so big that unless God intervenes he or she would fail. Throughout history the people who have had the greatest accomplishments had the biggest dreams, but also faced the greatest obstacles. Think about the dream that Martin Luther King Jr. had and the speech that he gave that described his dream. King's dream was big and his obstacles were great but he never gave up hope.

Foundation Number #2: Have faith in God

In the scriptures, Jeremiah 29:11, we read the following encouraging words: "For I know the plans that I have for you, says the Lord, Plans to give you hope and a future..." This passage shows us two things about God. One; He is in control. God has already mapped out your destiny and there is nothing that man can do to stop that. God sets us all at ease in Jeremiah 29:11 by letting us know that the map of our lives is filled with roads of hope. In your times of discouragement follow God, stick to his map and remain on his roads of hope by putting your faith in him. Two; no matter how bad things look, we need to know that God works for the good of those who love him (Romans 8:28). This simply means that God is your number one fan and that he is there to help you as you face every challenge.

Foundation Number #3: Develop a support system of good people

Coaches, teachers, parents, sisters, brothers, friends and/or religious leaders can all serve as part of your support system. There is much success to be found in family support and wise counsel. There is somebody out there who has been where you want to go and I'm sure that they would be willing to share with you what it takes to make it.

Foundation Number #4: Work hard

Train your body, mind, soul and spirit. To reach your dream hard work is inevitable. Your dream will demand discipline from you. I like to think of discipline as consistently putting your knowledge into action. Discipline must be implemented in every part of your life. Why? Because on your way to accomplishing your dream every part of your life will be tested and challenged. Sooner or later the thing that separates those who have accomplished their dreams and those who have not will be the discipline of hard work.

Foundation Number #5: Never quit.

If you never quit, you will never lose! Countless people throughout history spend their childhood days dreaming of what they want to be when they grow up. Later in life, these same people find themselves bruised and battered by the obstacles that stand in the way of their dreams. Some of them will succeed and others will fail. The difference will be how they react to the pressure.

It's crucial in life to understand the difference between being knocked down and being knocked out. To be knocked down is not a bad thing. It simply means you've fallen but you've made a decision to get back up and keep moving toward your dream. To be knocked out means you have fallen and for whatever reason, you are going to stay down, perhaps with your dream just out of reach.

I am convinced that God has given you great dreams that you are fully capable of achieving as long as you never quit! Regardless of what you have or don't have, you can succeed! Regardless of whether your parents are there for you or not you can succeed! Regardless of race or gender, you can succeed! Never quit and you will achieve your dreams!

Contact Brian Pruitt to speak at your next event.

If you would like Brian Pruitt to come and speak at your next event here are a few ways to contact us.

Brian is great for:
- Corporate Meetings
- Church's
- Colleges
- School Assemblies
- Sports Teams
- Men's Conferences
- Youth Conferences

Brian Pruitt Motivational is your fit.

Address:

Brian Pruitt Motivational
P.O. Box 294
Saginaw, MI 48606
Phone: (989) 249-0951
E-Mail: brianpruitt41@hotmail.com

To find out more about Brian Pruitt Motivational please go to our web site.

www.pruittmotivational.com
www.haccman.com